WINTER HARVEST
COOKBOOK

WINTER HARVEST COOKBOOK

How to Select and Prepare
Fresh Seasonal Produce
All Winter Long

LANE MORGAN

SASQUATCH BOOKS

Library of Congress Cataloging-in-Publication Data
Morgan, Lane, 1949–
   Winter harvest cookbook: how to select and prepare fresh seasonal produce
   all winter long / Lane Morgan.
      p.   cm.
   Includes bibliographical references.
   Includes index.
   ISBN 0-912365-35-8 (pbk.): $14.95
   1. Cookery (Vegetables)   I. Title.
TX801.M68   1990   90-47422
641.6'5—dc20   CIP

Design by Kris Morgan
Cover illustration by Don Baker
Interior illustrations by Celeste Henriquez
Composition by Scribe Typography

Published by Sasquatch Books
1931 Second Avenue
Seattle, WA 98101
(206) 441-5555

For Bruce

ACKNOWLEDGMENTS

I am grateful to many people for encouragement and recipe suggestions. Besides those named elsewhere I want to thank Mary Anderson, Trey Walker, Otto Goldschmid, and Carolyn Marr. Binda Colebrook, Gretchen Hoyt, Ben Craft, and Mark Musick all furthered my education in the realities of local agriculture. Anne Depue and Chad Haight at Sasquatch Books are fun to work with, and Alice Copp Smith is a wonderfully patient editor. My husband, Bruce Brown, and our daughters, Laurel and Deshanna, were frontline taste-testers for hundreds of recipes.

CONTENTS

INTRODUCTION

This book got its start more than 10 years ago, when I first encountered Binda Colebrook's *Winter Gardening in the Maritime Northwest*. I liked the idea of extending my gardening season, and I began some tentative experiments in my backyard in Seattle. When we moved to the country in 1979, I learned to my delight that Binda lived and farmed nearby. We became friends, and I helped with the research for the second edition of *Winter Gardening*.

Under her tutelage my winter garden flourished, but then I had a new problem. What was I supposed to do with all that chard and kale and salsify? Customers at the Bellingham Farmers Market, where I sold my surplus, had the same trouble. A lumpy Jerusalem artichoke, however sweet and crisp, somehow doesn't inspire the kind of culinary confidence that comes from a perfect, vine-ripe tomato. But on the other hand, a perfect Jerusalem artichoke is available and affordable in Bellingham in December, while a good tomato is not.

I began to hunt up recipes for my new crops, and to invent a few of my own. The process was very satisfying. For one thing, I have more patience for cooking in winter. Since I can't garden in the dark, I might as well be inside. For another, food seems more important then. We want to gather our friends at the table and keep the gloom away. I feel victorious when I come back from the muddy garden, clutching a bunch of leeks and chard, ready for adventure.

Why winter vegetables

Everything tastes best in its season. Whether your produce is from your garden or from the market, the best value for your money, your palate, and your health is in the crops that flourish most naturally. In summer, this is easy advice to follow. Who wouldn't choose fresh raspberries over stored apples in July? In winter, what used to be an inescapable cycle of seasonal food has begun to seem an exercise in self-discipline. It's hard not to be seduced by the ever-increasing array of produce from someone else's summer. But locally grown Brussels sprouts, properly cooked, really will taste better than corn trucked in from Florida.

Furthermore, the more local our food, the better we can assess its real costs and benefits. For example, nearly half the tomatoes sold in the United States between December and May come from the Culiacán Valley in Mexico. Americans want their produce spotless—especially when they are paying top dollar—so the tomatoes (and the workers who harvest them) are repeatedly and heavily sprayed with pesticides and fungicides. Then the tomatoes are picked green, bathed in chlorine, gassed with ethylene to stimulate reddening (but not ripening), and shipped across the continent, losing vitamins every step of the way.

When these tomatoes end up on the shelf in Seattle, they are still legally fresh, but they are neither tasty nor nutritious, and they may not even be safe. Assuming that they actually have been tested for violations of pesticide regulations—and that's not a safe assumption—they will have gone into the salad long before the lab reports are in. If the price tag on those tomatoes included the real costs in health and environmental damage, the product would be a lot less alluring. (Long-distance organic produce, though preferable, is not likely to rate much better nutritionally.)

Fortunately, there is no need to put purity before pleasure at the dinner table. When it comes to winter produce, good sense and good taste go together.

What winter vegetables

The vegetables featured in this book reach their peak of flavor in cool weather. Corn, tomatoes, eggplant, green beans, peppers, and zucchini are all fruits and seeds, the crown of the plant's creation. It takes a lot of energy to produce them, and that energy comes from long, sunny days. When the nights are long and the days are cool, most plants forgo flowers and stick with the basics: leaves and roots. Spinach, lettuce, cauliflower, mustard in its infinite varieties, kale and collards, and leeks reach culinary perfection before they flower. If their development is hurried along by too much light and heat, their vitality will suffer along with their flavor. Spindly little summer lettuces and spinach are likely to bolt to seed before they reach edible size.

Beets, carrots, parsnips, salsify, scorzonera, celeriac, and others are biennials. Their roots store the nutrients that will get the dormant plants through the winter. In many cases cold weather improves the taste, converting some of the starches in the roots to sugar. If they don't end up on your table first, the plants will draw from these high-energy reserves come spring to produce flowers and seeds.

Crops such as winter squash, potatoes, and yams mostly ripen in summer, but unlike tomatoes or green beans, they actually are improved in many cases by some time in storage.

This book is dedicated to the pleasures of fresh food in the winter season. But I admit that even in the Pacific Northwest, which is a mecca for cool-weather crops, total fidelity to a fresh regional table would be pretty restrictive. After all, cardboard tomatoes sell not because anybody really likes them, but because people crave an alternative to rutabagas. I'm not willing to do without lemons and oranges, winter or summer, and many of my favorite recipes call for canned tomatoes. Though fashion may scorn it, canned and frozen produce is often a better choice than globe-trotting "fresh." A tomato that was picked ripe and canned will be just as tasty cooked as one that was picked green and shipped, at a fraction of the price. (The vitamin C will be long gone in either case.) Likewise, fresh spinach is no nutritional powerhouse unless it's locally grown and you plan to eat it within a day or two. Otherwise, buy frozen and save yourself the cleaning time. Or skip spinach until you can find some worth eating.

All cooking was seasonal until recent times, so winter vegetables are central to many classic recipes. French *garbure*, Italian *bagna cauda*, Brazilian *feijoada*, Japanese *tsukemono*—all are based on cold-weather stalwarts like cabbage, cardoons, collards, and turnips. A vegetable like kale reveals an amazing number of uses and attributes as it moves from the "brose" soups of Scotland to the *caldo verde* of Portugal to the stews of Central Africa, and across the ocean to Southern soul food. Other standard winter staples—including potatoes, yams, and rutabagas—have a much greater culinary range than most of us know.

The many gardeners who have been inspired by *Winter Gardening* and other guides have been active in reviving old recipes and inventing new ones. As every gardener knows, a bumper crop can be a potent source of inspiration.

I have tried to keep esoteric ingredients and complicated procedures to a minimum. If you garden, you have already done plenty of work before the food hits the kitchen, and if you live in a rural area as I do, you can't just run down to the corner if the recipe calls for a dash of Pernod. On the other hand, I love trying new tastes. Moroccan pickled lemons won't be easy to find at the store, but they are simple and cheap to prepare.

Where to get them

The more familiar winter vegetables can be found in any supermarket. Whenever possible, buy produce that is locally grown. You will get fresher, higher-quality products, and you will be investing in the future of agriculture in your region. As a local buyer, you also have more power. Complaints and suggestions from consumers reach the local farmer in a hurry.

Keep in mind that local does not necessarily mean dirt cheap. Growing crops for winter harvest takes skill. Harvesting them is cold, wet, dirty work. Farmers aren't going to do it if it doesn't pay. Unlike meat and grain—the true production costs of which are obscured by irrigation subsidies and other political hat tricks—locally produced vegetables have to pay their own way. Eating in season is still economical, but don't expect giveaway prices.

Specialty stores and farmers markets are good sources of lesser-known or highly perishable foods. Some small-scale growers will produce on contract: you commit yourself at planting time to a certain number of celeriacs and pick them up in the fall.

If you are a gardener, consider extending your season. Proper attention to vegetable varieties and planting times can give you salads in November and leeks in March. Gardeners in many regions can harvest vegetables every day of the year, and cold frames and greenhouses make winter crops possible even in severe climates. Apartment dwellers can keep themselves in salads with some pots in a sunny window.

I live just south of the Canadian border in Sumas, Washington, where the murky winter weather common to the maritime Northwest is enlivened every year or two with screaming winds and zero-degree blizzards. A more typical January day might have eight hours of feeble daylight and a high temperature of 20°F. Nevertheless, between November and April my garden has produced broccoli, Brussels sprouts, kale, collards, various cabbages, leeks, green onions, leaf celery, Swiss chard, lettuce, endive, spinach, sorrel, cauliflower, Jerusalem artichokes, cardoons, celeriac, parsnips, salsify, and more. Other late crops, such as potatoes, carrots, and winter squash, are stored inside, away from pests and frosts. I certainly don't raise all those vegetables every year, but I can nearly always count on something.

Because winter plants are hardy, it isn't surprising that many of them flourish on their own. Burdock, chicory, nettles, fennel, and dandelions are all welcome additions to winter or early spring meals, and I have seen all of them growing in vacant lots in Seattle as well as in the countryside.

Kitchen equipment

None of these recipes requires a lot of special equipment. I don't have a food processor or a microwave oven, and the only electric kitchen appliance I use regularly is a blender. I do use a mortar and pestle, and a great big food mill—the kind that makes applesauce by the gallon. Since my kitchen is small and I usually work at home, I probably have less counter space and more cooking time than a lot of people, and that naturally affects my techniques. I'm not crusading against labor-saving devices—by all means use them if you've got them—but rather than passing on untested instructions, I will assume you can adapt my low-tech way of doing things to your own kitchen.

PRODUCE LIST

AMARANTH
Amaranthus spp.

As amaranth, this fleshy green or reddish potherb has been enjoying a modest renaissance, particularly for the nutritional virtues of its tiny seeds. As pigweed, amaranth is still the same old garden weed it ever was. It is up early in the spring, and the young leaves are a reasonable substitute for spinach. As they get tougher and stronger tasting, leaves should be treated like chard. I add the odd bit of amaranth to stir-fries and mixed-green dishes such as hortopita.

There is no reason a gardener should ever have to buy amaranth for greens; unless you run a very tight ship, you are bound to have some around. Nongardeners can look for it in Asian markets as *een choi*, or in Latin markets as *bledo* or *alegría*. Commercial seed is worth it if you want to grow grain. An ornamental variety, often sold in flower catalogs as a giant Love Lies Bleeding, has red leaves that look lovely in a spring salad. Amaranth is an excellent vegetable source of calcium and iron.

APPLES
Mutsu, Melrose, Idared

Cold storage and selective breeding have made apples available all year round. The problem is that many of them don't taste very good, even eaten fresh. Cooking apples need even more flavor if they are to provide anything more than bulk to a recipe. Fortunately, small orchards and nurseries are reviving many long-keeping, great-tasting varieties. Apple trees don't have to take up a lot of room. Dwarf varieties will grow in a half barrel on the patio.

ARUGULA
garden rocket, misticanza
Eruca sativa

Documentation of arugula in the kitchen goes back to at least the late medieval period. After a recent period of intense trendiness, it seems to have settled into a modest popularity as a salad green. I love the sesame-pepper taste of the young plants, especially when mixed with the blander corn salad that grows

AMARANTH

nearby in my winter garden. The big plants are too hot to eat, but if you leave a few for seed you'll have arugula all spring and fall.

When buying arugula, look for bright green, young plants; wash them gently and thoroughly, and use right away. Dry the leaves gently; they can't take rough handling.

BEETS
Beta vulgaris

Spring is the time for succulent little baby beets, steamed, with a little butter. In the fall, you want types that hold their sugar content well and do not develop a woody core. Gardeners can experiment with mangel-wurzel and other sugar-beet types, which are huge, hardy, and very sweet. Young beet greens are deservedly popular in the kitchen. The larger ones, if not too weatherbeaten, can be substituted for chard. In fact they are chard—simply a bulbous-rooted variety. That explains why chard is called spinach beet in Britain and silver beet in Australia. Beets are high in calcium, vitamin A, thiamine, and riboflavin. Italian cooking makes imaginative use of beets, incorporating them into ravioli and antipasti. Microwave ovens, which streamline the time-consuming baking that precedes many old recipes, may bring more of these recipes into North American kitchens. Salt will take the red stain off your hands.

BROCCOLI
Brassica deracea

Supermarket broccoli just scratches the surface of the types available to the gardener. Overwintering varieties allow a harvest in early spring. Most of these are of the cut-and-come-again type. After harvesting the central stalk, which may be green, white, or even purple, you can keep cutting side shoots until they are too small to bother with. The last straggly shoots are good additions to stir-fries; they are sweet and nutritious and they cook in an instant.

Shoppers should insist on deep-green, tight heads of broccoli. In the garden, however, heads that are bolting into flower are worth bringing to the kitchen and steaming lightly. They provide a peppery overlay to the sweetness of fresh broccoli.

ARUGULA

Corn salad and arugula with beets

Green salads

Broccoli is wonderfully versatile in the kitchen, and it's one of the most healthful things you can eat. Its adaptability to a range of climates also means that it shows up in a great many cuisines, from Italian to Chinese. British recipes and seed catalogs may refer to "Calabrese"; that's regular green broccoli in the United States.

BRUSSELS SPROUTS
Brassica oleracea var. *gemifera*

Brussels sprouts are at their best in winter, as frost sweetens them. Hardy European varieties can stand bitter weather; I have broken through frozen snow to harvest them and seen them survive the thaw to produce some more. Whether buying or harvesting, look for tight, green buttons of medium size, and once you have them in your kitchen, *do not overcook*. Most Brussels-sprout haters got that way from an encounter with the pale, rank-tasting victims of too much boiling. Try steaming or sautéing instead.

If you grow your own, don't spurn the elongating heads as the plants go to flower in the spring. They have a slightly peppery taste and are delicious in stir-fries or quickly steamed and drizzled with butter and lemon.

CABBAGE
Brassica spp.

Cabbages take a bewildering array of forms, and they are cool-weather crops par excellence. Herewith an informal grouping:

Asian types

Large, crisp, mild-tasting Chinese or nappa cabbage (*Brassica pekinensis* var. *cylindrica*) is sort of the iceberg lettuce of the cabbage family. It shares another characteristic in that it is tricky to grow, and I have given up trying. Fortunately, it is widely available. Individual heads tend to be huge, but it keeps fairly well under refrigeration, so don't hesitate. Any excess can be made into *kim chee*.

Bok choy and its cousins, with pale, thick stalks and dark green leaves, have a bit more flavor and are easier to grow because they do not need to form a head.

BOK CHOY

Fish soup from Fujian

Seed catalogs and Asian markets will introduce you to an ever-growing array of other types, shading by flavor and species into the mustards, which I have arbitrarily gathered into a separate section (*see* mustards). In general, the larger and paler the produce, the milder the taste, so you might tailor your experiments accordingly.

European types

Savoy cabbage—Exceptionally hardy and very beautiful, savoys are one of the best arguments for a winter garden. They are not often seen in supermarkets in this country, since their long growing season and relatively short shelf life make them problematic for agribusiness, but they are troupers in the garden. The crinkled ("savoyed") leaves evidently provide some cold protection (savoy spinach is also a winter variety). The flavor is milder and the leaves less fibrous than those of ordinary cabbage. Not recommended for a mayonnaise-laden coleslaw, but otherwise you can try it in most recipes calling for cabbage. It is especially nice for stuffed cabbage because the softer leaves are easier to handle without breaking.

Red cabbage—A cross section of red cabbage is so lovely, it's worth getting one just for that. Its beauty is a factor when used fresh in salads. Red cabbages tend to be a bit firmer and harder than their green counterparts and may require longer cooking if tenderness is the issue.

Green cabbage—Shoppers look for hard, firm heads of cabbage, medium-sized rather than huge. A big one might be dominated by a huge core, and you won't know until you've cut it open. Gardeners have the option of fast-maturing, loose-headed spring cabbage, but these varieties seldom make it to market.

CARDOONS
Cynara cardunculus

Food historian Waverley Root says that European women in the Middle Ages ate cardoons to assure the birth of a boy. I eat them for the artichoke-like taste. Cardoons are a giant form of thistle, related to artichokes but hardier and—because one eats the stems instead of the flower buds—more prolific. They are beginning to find their way into gourmet markets in the Pacific Northwest.

Cardoons are most common in Northern Italian cooking, and have immigrated along with Italians to Argentina, where they are widely served. They are used in *bagna cauda* and other traditional dishes. I have read that the Italian kind is milder in flavor than the type I have been able to find, which requires blanching in the garden and again in the kitchen.

CARDOONS

Beef with cardoons and mushrooms

Cardoons à la Lyonnaise

Stewed cardoons

Angelo Pellegrini has raised cardoons successfully for many years in his Seattle garden, and he makes an eloquent case for them in his fine book *The Food Lover's Garden*. A happy cardoon can get six feet tall and five feet across, so don't try them on your miniature patio. Pellegrini also cooks with the ubiquitous Canadian thistle, which Italians know as wild cardoon. I haven't tried this. Cardoon stalks will keep a week refrigerated in a plastic bag. Strip and trim the stalks before cooking. The central ones are the mildest.

CARROTS
Dauca carota

If you garden, you can indulge in the great range of carrot sizes and flavors and plan your menus according to type. Storage and winter-hardy carrots, sad to say, are just not as succulent as their less sturdy summer brethren. However, even marginal offerings can be put to good use in curries and other strongly flavored dishes, provided they are still firm and not woody.

CAULIFLOWER
Brassica oleracea botrytis

Home gardeners have a tremendous range of cauliflowers to choose from. If you are determined, you can eat them almost continuously from September to April.

Shoppers should look for the obvious: firm heads that have not begun to separate or discolor. I can't tell any consistent difference in taste between the modest heads and the gargantuan ones, so let convenience be your guide. Specialty cauliflowers—green or golden or purple—are beginning to crop up in the stores. They all taste more or less the same. You could take advantage of these plant breeders' fantasies for an eye-catching antipasto plate. The purple ones turn green when cooked.

CELERIAC

Celeriac and shrimp with mustard dressing

Celeriac rémoulade

Stuffed celeriac

CELERIAC
celery-root
Apium graveolens var. *rapaceum*

A member of the parsley family (as is celery), celeriac is grown for its bulbous root. It has a mild flavor, rather like the blanched heart of a regular celery. I wish it well as a supermarket vegetable, since it is slow to grow and hard to clean, two drawbacks for the home gardener. It keeps well, though, and the size is more convenient than those massive storebought celery bunches that inevitably grow limp in the back of my refrigerator.

Small, gnarly roots are good for soups and stews. If you grow or buy nice big ones, you can try the many Continental recipes for purées and rémoulades.

CELERY
Apium graveolens

Leaf celery, available from some European seed catalogs, is surprisingly hardy. With a little mulching, it will survive all but the fiercest Northwest winters and produce new growth in early spring. The flavor is much stronger than that of commercial celery. Too much can overpower your pot roast, and munching it raw is out of the question. Cut recipe amounts in half if you are using home-grown leaves.

CHESTNUTS
Castenea spp.

Commercial chestnut culture is making a modest comeback in North America, using Asian and European varieties that are resistant to the blight that eliminated our native trees. If you have your own trees (you need two for pollination) you may be rolling in bounty.

Despite their rich, mealy taste, chestnuts are low in fat, providing their calories in the form of complex carbohydrates. They are versatile, moving with ease from soups to risottos to desserts. Chestnut flour, seldom seen in this country, is used in Italian cakes and pastries.

Chestnuts are perishable and they aren't cheap, so plan your purchases carefully. Look for firm, full nuts. Light weight and a blackened skin are signs of spoilage. Large nuts lessen the labor of peeling.

CHICORY

Italian greens and rice soup

Baked fish and chicory

Campania pizza

CHICORY

Cichorium endiva var. *crispa*

The nomenclature for chicory and its relatives is confusing, to say the least. Common names have undergone strange transmutations as they traveled from European kitchens, so that the Brussels (or Witloof) chicory they serve in Brussels is better known here as Belgian endive, and the French *chicorée frisée* is sold in the U.S. as curly endive. The glamorous red radicchios are also chicories (or endives), as is escarole. Heirloom American recipes calling for "succory" also mean chicory. Check your recipe carefully for clues before you harvest or shop.

For purposes of this book, chicory is a curly- or toothy-leaved, loose-headed plant with a characteristic bitter tang. It is highly regarded as a salad green, and I think it's even better cooked. The garden plants are robust and hardier than lettuce, although constant rain discourages them. If you give them some shelter from the rain, they will thrive and sweeten through the first frosts of winter, resulting in better taste than you can buy. They keep well in a plastic bag in the refrigerator, with the added benefit that the bitterness moderates with time. The central leaves are paler and milder than the outer ones, allowing the cook to employ variations on the basic taste theme. (*See also* endive, escarole, *and* radicchio.)

COLLARDS

Brassica oleracea var. *acephala*

Primitive members of the cabbage family, collards are among the most forgiving of garden plants. Cool-weather gardeners like them for their hardiness; they also hold up better in hot climates than their more refined cousins. Even the most moribund-looking January collard may revive to produce new greens in March, so don't be too quick to put them out of their misery.

Since collards will live through most anything, you can hardly expect them to be delicate in flavor or texture. The leaves are tough and the flavor is assertive. They go well with beef and pork and add authority to winter soups. They are an excellent vegetable source of calcium and are also high in vitamins A and C.

When shopping for collards, look for deep green—not yellowish—leaves and firm stems. Collards are never crisp, but they should not be limp and floppy.

COLLARDS

Caldo verde

Ethiopian collards and cottage cheese

CORN SALAD
field lettuce, lamb's tongue, mâche, feldsalat
Valerianella eriocarpa

I used to find corn salad distressingly bland, but I've come around. Its soft taste and texture make a good foil for more pungent winter greens. This is a venerable and popular European market plant, with literary cachet: it was the green Rapunzel's mother craved in the Grimms' fairy tale. It's easy to grow, although care must be taken in harvest because the leaves are soft and its ground-hugging habit makes it prone to dirt. Unbruised plants will keep about a week under refrigeration. Corn salad does double duty in the garden, serving as a good winter ground cover and green manure crop.

DANDELIONS
Taraxacum officinale

In earliest spring, dandelion fanciers dot their yards with upended flower pots to blanch the young growth of their favorite weed. Commercial seed, available through gourmet garden catalogs, produces a less bitter green, but I doubt the difference is worth the expense. Seeds marketed as "Italian dandelion" are actually a form of chicory. Dandelion greens are used primarily in salads. They are very nutritious, though not usually eaten in such quantities as to make that a major issue. They don't keep well.

Although the roots have the stronger effect, the leaves are also a diuretic (note the French common name, *pissenlit*).

ENDIVE
Belgian endive, Witloof chicory
Cichorium intybus

In this book, we use the name endive to mean the delicacy, resembling a pale, miniature head of romaine lettuce, that is served at outrageous prices in French restaurants. This *chicon* is produced by digging up the roots of the summer-sown plants in the fall, storing them in the dark, and harvesting the doomed, blanched

FLORENCE FENNEL

Braised Florence fennel

Florence fennel and apple salad

Florence fennel au gratin

shoots that result. A disciplined gardener can get an impressive supply for the cost of a packet of seed. That may be the only way you are likely to get enough endive to cook for company. Shoppers (unless cost is no object) are better off sticking to salads, where the leaves go further.

An endive *chicon* will keep for several days in the refrigerator. Don't wash it before storage, and keep it dark. The core is the most bitter. You can remove it with a paring knife if you want a milder flavor. (*See also* chicory.)

ESCAROLE
Cichorium endiva

A broad-leaved variety of chicory, escarole resembles a large, blowsy romaine. The flavor is similar to chicory, but the leaves are fleshier. Full-heart Batavian is the most common variety. The heart referred to is the blanched, delicious center, which is sweet with just enough bitter edge to be interesting. Escarole and chicory can be used interchangeably in most recipes. Like chicory, escarole tastes best after a frost, so Northwest-grown crops are preferable to California and Florida imports. (*See also* chicory.)

FLORENCE FENNEL
finocchio dolce
Fœniculum vulgare

A lovely plant with feathery leaves and a fist-sized bulbous base, it resembles an elegant celery and is available in both green and bronze varieties. Both leaves and base are used, the former mostly in salads and as a garnish for fish and pork. The mild anise flavor adapts to a variety of treatments.

Shoppers should look for fresh-looking greens and firm, medium-sized bulbs. Try to buy whole plants rather than just bulbs. You get more value, and you can judge the freshness by the leaves. Large, stringy bulbs can be deveined like celery. The bulbs keep fairly well refrigerated in a plastic bag; the greens should be used right away.

GOBO

Kimpira gobo

Gobo wrapped with beef

GOBO
burdock
Arctium spp.

This is the same plant as cocklebur, whose pricky, tenacious seeds were the inspiration for Velcro. It is large, deep-rooted, and nearly indestructible once established, so I hesitate to recommend it as a garden plant unless you are far more organized and disciplined than I am. On the other hand, the taste is among the best of all winter roots: full and rich, with a bittersweet edge. Besides its culinary value, Japanese gobo (*Arctium lappa*) is widely taken in Japan to improve strength and virility, and the naturalized American varieties are used in a number of herbal remedies. You often can find gobo in Asian markets and specialty groceries.

The dark brown root is the most important culinary part. It is long—up to 18 inches—and slender; you will need to dig it, not pull it. Although the young leaves are sometimes used as a green, I find them unpleasantly hairy and bitter.

GOOD KING HENRY
mercury
Chenopodium bonus henricus

I have ordered seed for this heirloom potherb, but I have yet to grow any. Plants are available from some nurseries. It is one of the roster of vigorous perennials, like sorrel and mint, that reappear in early spring and are relished accordingly. Young leaves can be substituted for spinach and chard. Stalks are steamed like asparagus. I like the flavor of its smaller relative, lamb's-quarters.

HAMBURG PARSLEY
turnip-rooted parsley
Petroselenium crispum var. *tuberosum*

A variety of parsley grown for its root, which looks like a small, dingy carrot and has a nice parsley taste. It's very good in stews and hearty soups and has many uses in folk medicine. The strong-flavored leaves can be substituted, sparingly, for regular parsley.

Gardeners can leave the plants in the ground through the winter. Shoppers should look for crisp, solid roots and store them like carrots. They will keep for a week or two.

JERUSALEM ARTICHOKES

Rutachoke salad

Soup Provençale

Turkish cauliflower and lentil stew

JERUSALEM ARTICHOKES
sunchoke, topinambour
Helianthus tuberosum

If you grow Jerusalem artichokes, you probably have more than you can eat. These prolific members of the sunflower family (the name Jerusalem is probably a corruption of the Italian *girasole*, "sun-turning") are among the hardiest of vegetables, surviving and multiplying though summer droughts and winter blizzards. John Goodyer, a young English botanist who received two tubers of the New World curiosity in 1617, reported that they increased a hundredfold in his garden. "I stocked Hampshire," he noted in his journal.

Once harvested, the thin-skinned tubers need careful handling. Buy only firm, fresh-looking specimens and refrigerate promptly.

Jerusalem artichokes are a boon to dieters and diabetics because they are low in calories and, when fresh, contain no starch at all, storing their carbohydrates in the form of inulin. They also are a good source of niacin and thiamine. They have a sweet, clean taste, slightly reminiscent of a real artichoke but much lighter. I like them raw as snacks, grated into salads, or fried up like hashbrowns. They discolor quickly when cut, so sprinkle them with lemon juice or keep them in acidulated water if appearance is important.

Peeling them is a chore. I don't bother unless they are so knobby that they can't be cleaned by scrubbing. If peeling is necessary, steam the artichokes about 5 minutes, and much of the skin will slip off.

KALE
chou frisé
Brassica oleracea, B. campestris

Kale is the reason I started this book. Under Binda Colebrook's tutelage I produced some nice plants, and marveled as they survived everything a Sumas winter could dish out. The only trouble was that I didn't know what to do with them. I've since learned that kale was once so ubiquitous that in Scotland "kailyard" was synonymous with garden. Mixed with grain or potatoes, kale kept generations of smallholders healthy through the grim northern winters. Kale also can take the heat, and it shows up in a number of Turkish and North African dishes.

Kale varies considerably in sweetness and toughness, and if you are a gardener you can take advantage of its variety. Shoppers must take what the commercial

KOHLRABI

Kohlrabi salad

Baked kohlrabi and fennel

growers produce. Look for deep green, fresh-looking leaves. Kale keeps fairly well, so you can buy in quantity. Common sense should prevail in cooking: young, fresh leaves, especially new spring growth, are best for sautéed and stir-fried dishes, and older specimens are good for soups. Like broccoli and other cabbage cousins, kale produces savory flower stalks in the spring.

KOHLRABI

Brassica oleracea caulorapa

This is more a cool-weather crop than a real winter stalwart, at least where I live. It's good, though, and it keeps and travels well, so it's beginning to show up in more supermarkets. Also called Hungarian turnip, it is not a turnip but a cousin of broccoli and cauliflower, grown for its swollen stem rather than its florets. Kohlrabi can be served either raw or cooked and can be substituted for celeriac or turnip in most recipes. The purple and green varieties taste the same to me.

Look for firm, medium-sized globes with a healthy sheen. If they are pitted or spotty they've been around too long, and the really large ones may have a tough core. You have to peel them; a paring knife works better than a potato peeler.

LEEKS

Allium ampeloprasum var. *porrum*

Leeks are among the oldest cultivated vegetables, taking their name from the Old English word *leac*, or plant. English kitchen gardens were once called leek gardens, just as their Scotch counterparts were called kailyards. In folklore leeks are most associated with the Welsh, who wear them in their hats on St. David's Day, and consume them in cock-a-leekie soup, among other dishes.

Although market gardeners find that giant leeks sell the best, the smaller ones taste better. Pencil-sized leeks are sweeter and milder than green onions and make a fine addition to an antipasto plate. I keep a batch of small ones, stunted by the calculated neglect of not thinning them, for midwinter green-onion substitutes. Medium-sized ones are best for side dishes and and cooked salads. I use the monsters in vichyssoise or purées.

The white shaft of a leek is produced by hilling soil up around the growing plant to blanch it. It has a milder flavor than the green part, so the more subtle the dish, the less green you should use. The outer leaves are too stringy for good eating but can be added to stocks. A midwinter leek can look weatherbeaten and still taste fine, but you should discard any with a yellow or brown tinge to the stalk.

If you move a few overwintered leeks to the flower border in spring, they will shoot up three or four feet and reward you with dramatic balls of white or lavender flowers in July, and you can save your own seed for the following year.

LETTUCE
Latuca sativa

With a bit of planning and even a makeshift cold frame, most Pacific Northwesterners can have garden lettuce from April into December. I've been amazed at how hardy these tender-looking plants can be. It's worth it to seek out seed from catalogs catering to northern growers. Territorial, Nichols, and Johnny's Selected Seeds all have good offerings. You probably will be harvesting leaf by leaf in November and December, so this is not the time to plan for a big Caesar salad. A mixture of lettuce, spinach, and corn salad is a more practical expectation for midwinter.

If your problem is oversupply—a lot of sad-looking lettuce that is about to bolt in early spring—you can substitute lettuce for Chinese cabbage and other mild greens in stir-fries and soups. Take care not to overcook the tender leaves.

MUSTARDS
(Brassica spp.*)*

There is a bewildering assortment of garden mustards, not to mention the wild types found in nearly every vacant lot and yard. Since these brassicas crossbreed with enthusiasm and self-sow with abandon, there is no telling what hybrids will crop up in your garden next spring. Students of particular cuisines will want to track down specific types. Garden stores and catalogs are getting more and more sophisticated in their offerings, but the overlap of common names makes it hard to be positive what you are planting.

My personal culinary taxonomy divides mustards into Southern and Asian, and I usually grow some of each. "Southern mustards" are the large, strong-flavored types generally found in the supermarket next to the collards. They need longer cooking, preferably in the company of a ham hock. In my garden, tyfon, which is actually a cross between rape and turnip, fills the bill. I sow some in midsummer for big cooking greens and some in fall for winter salads.

Asian mustards (and cabbages—the distinction is often academic in the kitchen) come in amazing variety—*mizuna*, *santoh*, bok choy, *tatsoi*, green-in-snow, and on and on. These vary a lot. Some are grown as much for the stem as for the leaves and are very mild in flavor. Others are nearly all leaf and intensely "green" in taste. Some are very peppery, some hardly at all. Most of them are easy to grow, and many are small enough to raise in a narrow planter strip on a city lot. They make an excellent introduction to winter gardening, since they are easy and versatile.

Freshness is the key in purchasing mustard greens. The big tough ones will keep quite a while, but they quickly lose their sweetness and become merely hot and harsh.

NETTLE
Urtica spp.

Northwest natives were amazed when nettle soups began to appear at fancy prices in some Seattle restaurants. The ubiquitous stinging nettle is probably second only to the equally ubiquitous slug on the local hate list. However, cooking eliminates the sting, and nettles have a long and honorable history as a potherb. In his 18th-century tour of the Hebrides, Samuel Johnson reports sitting down to a bowl of nettle soup served on a cloth made of nettle fiber.

Northwest Indians made fishing nets and blanket warps out of nettle fiber—which should be a clue to one culinary drawback. Because the stalks become very fibrous indeed, nettles should be picked young, and only the leaves should be used in cooking. I use plants no more than six inches high for omelets and other greens. You have a little more leeway if you are making a purée.

Nettles are an early spring rather than a real winter plant. The late fall growth is too coarse to eat, and the first frost mows it down. But by late February in a mild year, the first new shoots can be found in city lots as well as rural woods. Keeping a patch trimmed will encourage tender new growth throughout the year, but I think they taste best in springtime. Wear rubber gloves for picking and cleaning.

NETTLE

Cream of nettle soup

Nettle omelet

Wild sorrel and nettle sauce

ORACHE
mountain spinach
Atriplex hortensis

A member of the goosefoot family, orache is an annual relative of another heirloom vegetable, Good King Henry. Red-leaved and yellow-leaved forms can be grown as ornamentals and will reseed themselves. Orache is used like spinach, although its leaves are tougher and its flavor is coarser. I like the plants, especially the red ones, and I often add a handful of leaves to the mess of greens, but I wouldn't go out of my way to grow it.

PARSNIPS
Pastinaca sativa

The introduction of the potato to Europe in the 18th century ended the parsnip's reign as the premier winter root. Until then parsnips were a northern staple, especially during Lent in Catholic countries, when their bulk and pronounced flavor could fill in for the missing meat. Parsnips are not as versatile in the kitchen nor as nutritious as the blander spud, and their long roots and even longer growing season make them more trouble in the garden. Another strike against them in the commercial world is that they don't taste their best until they have been through a freeze. The ones at the grocery store may therefore be pasty-tasting imitations of the ones you grow yourself.

Nevertheless, I like parsnips and willingly double-dig a small bed most years to grow them. In a winter when the northeasters destroy everything above ground, it's a comfort to think of the parsnips I can harvest when the soil thaws a bit.

Shop for parsnips as you would for carrots. Check for firmness, and leave the monsters back in the bin.

PEARS
Comice, Bosc, Highland, Seckel

The classic Bartlett pear has ripened and gone by the time cool weather comes. Winter shoppers will find Comices, Boscs, Anjous, and other varieties. Boscs and other hard-as-a-rock types should be saved for poaching. For fresh eating, invest

ORACHE

in buttery Comices, or try growing a Highland or El Dorado tree. If you grow your own, pay careful attention to the harvesting instructions for your variety. Some ripen on the tree; others must be picked green and stored before they are ready to eat.

POTATOES
Solanum tuberosum

The potato has come back into its own lately as a health food. It is a reasonable source of protein and vitamin C (half as much as an orange, if you eat the skin), and an excellent source of potassium, niacin, and thiamine. If your garden is small, you may begrudge the space taken by the sprawling vines. If you have the room, though, you can grow specialty types like Peruvian purple or Yellow Finn that are hard to find at the supermarket. Potatoes don't do well in the garden most winters; if they don't freeze or rot, they are likely to feed the slugs before you get to them. Harvest in the fall and store them, keeping in mind that unlike many commercial spuds, yours have not been treated with growth inhibitor and will answer nature's urging with a forest of sprouts come spring.

QUINCES
Cydonia oblonga

The ornamental quinces common to Northwest yards and gardens sometimes set fruit, but a culinary quince tree is taller (up to 20 feet) and bears a hard fruit about the size and shape of a pear. Quinces are yellow, orange, or green on the outside, with hard, grainy flesh ranging from white to orange. They ripen from late summer to late fall and keep well.

Quinces must be cooked. They are high in pectin, and in North America they are generally relegated to jellies and preserves, but they have many other uses. In Iran and Turkey, where the the species originated, they are added to slow-cooked meat dishes and also used in Turkish delight. A popular Spanish confection made of simmered and dried quince pulp and sugar probably has the same culinary roots as Turkish delight. The slight astringency of cooked quince also will enliven a prosaic apple crisp or poached pear dessert.

Quinces have a pronounced and pleasant fragrance when ripe. Sniff before you buy, handle gently, and refrigerate. Well-treated fruit will keep several weeks.

RAAB
rapa, broccoli raab
Brassica rapa ruvo

This small brassica resembles a slender broccoli. It's easy to grow and less prone to rot during rainy autumns than broccoli itself. It may be the answer for gardeners with limited space and a passion for broccoli flavor. Common in Italian, especially Tuscan, recipes, it can be replaced by small broccoli or a mixture of broccoli and mustard greens. Stalks require peeling. I've never seen it in the store, but I don't see why it shouldn't have commercial appeal.

RADICCHIO
red chicory, treviso
Cichorium intybus

A truly beautiful plant, radicchio is a variety of the same species that is forced for Belgian endive *chicon*. The spectacular red-and-white-striped leaves look like small lettuces. The Verona type is round; treviso is elongated, like a miniature romaine. It's popular in salads, either alone or mixed with milder greens for contrast in flavor and color, but I prefer it lightly cooked.

Radicchio is expensive, so choose each head carefully. It is not difficult to grow, although it's rather slow. Your garden heads may be looser and more strongly flavored than storebought ones.

RADISHES
Raphanus sativus

The small red salad radishes are not particularly hardy, although they are among the first crops to mature in the spring. Some of the French icicle varieties are also grown for their greens, but I have yet to try them.

Winter radishes, more common in Japanese and Chinese cooking, are usually represented in this country by daikon. They are used in a variety of ways, both pickled and fresh, and their thick white roots provide the image behind the Hawaiian insult "daikon leg." Daikon is a problem in many organic gardens because it is a favorite of the voracious cabbage rootfly maggot. I don't grow it, but I can usually find it in a local produce department. The roots tend to be huge, but they keep well in the refrigerator so they needn't go to waste.

ROSE HIPS
Rosa spp.

Old-fashioned rugosa rose varieties have the largest, best-tasting hips. As an added benefit, the plants are immune to practically all the ills that more refined roses are heir to. The individual flowers are not as impressive as those of a tea rose, but the mass effect is pleasant. Rose hips have a nice tart taste and lots of vitamin C, but the fruit is small and seedy. They are most commonly used in teas and jellies, where the seeds can be strained out. Rose hips should be harvested before a heavy freeze. Be sure that the plants have not been sprayed with insecticides or fungicides. If the bugs can't eat it, you shouldn't.

RUTABAGAS
swedes
Brassica napus var. *napobrassica*

Rutabagas don't get very good press. Like parsnips, they were mostly eclipsed by the arrival of the potato in Europe. Also like parsnips, they are much better homegrown because a light frost sweetens them. Even storebought rutabagas deserve a second look. They are good in many winter soups and purées, and they make nice pies and custards. I also have substituted them for part of the potatoes in gnocchi with good results, though I don't blame Italian purists for cringing at the thought.

SALSIFY
oyster plant
Tragopogon porrifolius

A popular 19th-century root, salsify is benefiting from the vogue for specialty vegetables. All simple treatments—steamed, sautéed, puréed, creamed, or glazed —are good and easy. Don't expect a true oyster taste, but the flavor is pleasantly

ROSE HIPS

Rose pear granita

different from that of parsnips, carrots, and rutabagas: fuller, I guess you could say, and not so sweet.

Salsify is easy to grow, although very slow, and it is extremely hardy. You do need loose soil since the roots are long and slender. The plants are biennial, and you can get larger specimens by harvesting the second year. The roots keep for weeks refrigerated in a plastic bag. They are not particularly attractive, being hairy and dingy white, but don't let that deter you. Neither are they crisp, even when first harvested, but they should not be limp. Go for the largest roots, or you may not have much left between the peeling and the core.

SCORZONERA
picridie
Scorzonera hispanica

Often referred to as black oyster plant, although it is a different genus. Like Jerusalem artichokes, scorzonera contains its carbohydrates in the form of inulin. The taste is similar enough to that of salsify to make the two interchangeable. The black skin must be peeled carefully unless you don't mind your purées looking muddy and strange.

SORREL
Rumex spp.

Members of the buckwheat family, wild sorrels are everywhere. Even the more refined French garden type is easy to grow—in fact, it's hard to get rid of once established.

Sorrel doesn't keep well. Use it the day it's bought or picked, and cook very lightly if at all; overcooked sorrel is mushy. (Don't use an aluminum or cast-iron pan, or the leaves will turn an unappetizing blackish brown.)

If you cut back rank summer growth in September, you will get a nice new crop of fall leaves that will keep producing until a heavy freeze. Then the spring crop will be up with the daffodils, providing wonderful, bright-tasting salads when you need them most. Another salad resource with similar flavor is oxalis, in either its green or reddish-leaved form.

SCORZONERA

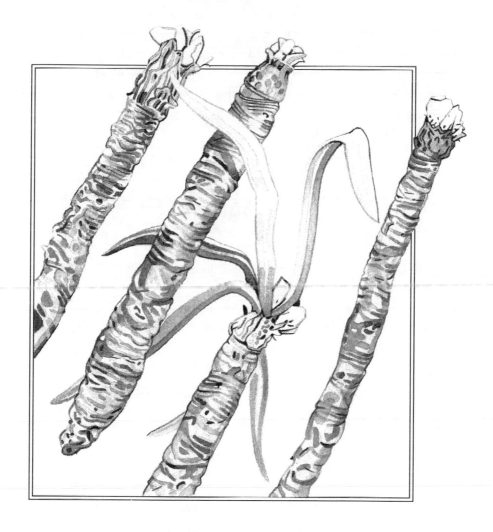

Le Gourmand salsify

Scorzonera with sour cream

SPINACH
Spinacea oleracea

Better to buy frozen spinach than some of the bedraggled, muddy bunches that turn up in markets in the winter. My garden spinach is harvested, leaf by precious leaf, for salads from November until February, when the plants begin to grow again. The winter production is scant, but the flavor is sensational; this is the sweetest, richest, best spinach salad you have ever tasted. I use storebought— fresh or frozen—for cooked dishes.

SQUASH
Cucurbita spp.

Winter squashes can induce a lot of guilt in nutrition-oriented cooks. They are so healthy, so high in fiber, so full of vitamin A. But most people just don't find their bland sweetness very appealing, and few modern families can cope with a 20-pound Hubbard. Both of these problems can be overcome. Delicatas, Japanese Kabochas, and other types are now bred to serve one or two people instead of a dozen or more. A fresh Delicata is a revelation if you have been avoiding squash for a decade or two. The other big improvement is in recipes. Japanese, African, and other cuisines make inventive and flavorful use of these New World vegetables.

Home gardeners should note that unlike most storage crops, squashes like a bit of warmth as well as dryness. I cure mine on top of the kitchen cabinets. Also, despite the old line about the frost on the pumpkin, it's better to bring them in before a freeze. Most squashes store well, but some hold their flavor much better than others. Delicatas, pumpkins, and acorn and spaghetti squashes are all close relatives of summer zucchini and pattypans, and they are best eaten within a month or two. They get blander and more fibrous as the winter wears on. Butter-cups, Butternuts, Hubbards, and Japanese Kuris and Kabochas belong to different species and stay sweet and smooth much longer.

SWEET POTATOES AND YAMS
Ipomoea batatas

I always hated sweet potatoes until I learned that they go better with soy sauce than with melted marshmallows. They are very high in vitamin A, and all they require is a bit of thought to keep their sweetness from being cloying. They don't grow well here, but they are easy to buy and they will keep for months if the storage temperature does not fall much below 50°F. (I once stashed a bagful in my chilly pantry and they promptly rotted.) Grocery store sweet potatoes and yams are just different varieties of the same plant. The true yam (*Dioscorea* spp.) is a starchy tropical root that tastes more like a potato.

SWISS CHARD
spinach beet
Beta vulgaris var. *cicla*

Chard is tough and prolific, probably the most reliable winter green in terms of production. I value it more each year: It fills the gap when my spinach is barely holding its own, and it substitutes for a number of more perishable greens. Provençal and Spanish cuisines make especially good use of chard.

I think green chard tastes better than the undeniably beautiful ruby variety. In any case, whether buying or harvesting, pick firm, resilient stalks. If you are going to use the stalks, look for the broad types rather than the ones that resemble beet greens; they are less stringy and easier to handle on the dinner plate. Gardeners interested in growing for stalks should look for French chard, Lucullus, or Large White-Ribbed varieties.

Give some thought to matching the chard to the recipe. New spring growth is fine with brief cooking and light seasoning. Big tattered December leaves had better go into soup or lasagne. Chard leaves can be stuffed like cabbage, with the same fillings.

Chard keeps fairly well in the refrigerator, and stalks can be saved for a week or so until you have enough for a separate recipe. Good crisp stalks can also stand in for cooked (not raw) celery.

TURNIPS
Brassica rapa

Turnips have been cultivated since prehistoric times, and their sturdiness has made them a vegetable of last resort, to be fed to the stock when times are good and brought to the table when times are bad. Carved and lighted, they were also the precursor of the jack-o'-lantern pumpkin.

Turnips are particularly esteemed in French and Japanese cooking. Small, quick-growing types are steamed or sautéed. Big winter keepers are best for stews, purées, and Japanese pickles. Turnip sticks are a popular companion to carrot sticks for after-school snacks at our house.

Rootfly maggots love turnips, so I don't often grow them. If I did, I would seek out the Japanese types. Turnip greens are also a welcome addition to the mustard family.

YAMS
See Sweet Potatoes.

OTHER INGREDIENTS

CITRUS FRUITS

Oranges, lemons, and limes never are in season in the Pacific Northwest, but they are at their best during our winter. I use organically grown (or at least unsprayed) oranges or lemons in all recipes calling for grated peel. Government-authorized safe consumption levels for the many chemicals used on citrus crops are based on the fruit, not on the peel that actually receives the spray. Fortunately, many supermarkets, as well as food co-ops and health food stores, now stock organic fruit. Organic oranges taste better too. My guess is that in the absence of chemically enhanced coloring, the organically grown crops are allowed to ripen longer on the tree.

TOMATOES

Canned tomatoes are usually the best choice for winter cooking. Fresh ones, even when they aren't pale orange and hard as baseballs, are nearly always a disappointment. Plum tomatoes are relatively low in moisture and hold their texture better canned than do beefsteak types. I don't like to can, so I freeze or dry any surplus tomato harvest.

Freezing tomatoes is ridiculously easy and preserves true fresh tomato taste, though at the expense of texture. Just wash some perfect ripe tomatoes, dry thoroughly, and pop into the freezer in a plastic bag—no blanching or peeling necessary. Remove from the freezer half an hour before you need them. They will look just like fresh tomatoes and feel like icy little bowling balls. Remove skin by placing them in a bowl of warm water for about 30 seconds. The skin will crack and then slip smoothly off.

The thawed tomatoes will be watery and mushy. You can't slice them for a salad, but they are just fine—better than anything you can buy—in a blender salsa or a lightly cooked soup.

Dried tomatoes are easy to make at home if you have a food dryer or a gas oven. The imported dried tomatoes that sell for sensational prices are sun-dried (or so the label claims), but the principle is the same. Take firm, ripe tomatoes. Wash and dry them, then slice into rounds about a quarter-inch thick. Place on drying racks over a steady, gentle heat source. Dry until stiff and very chewy (about two days with my food dryer). Pry the translucent slices off the rack. They can be kept in a sealed jar or plastic bag or, more glamorously, in a jar of olive oil with some sliced garlic and a few leaves of basil.

They are great in stews and soups, as a last-minute addition to sautéed leeks or broccoli, on pizzas, in steamed rice, and on sandwiches. They are hard to cut with a knife; use scissors instead. The flavored olive oil is perfect in salad dressings.

RICE

Only a fraction of the hundreds of varieties of rice grown around the world are available in North America, but they are enough to create confusion nonetheless. Different cuisines value different properties in this highly versatile staple. Sushi and other Japanese dishes work best with short-grain "sticky rice." Arborio rice, the short-grain, starchy Italian variety favored for risottos, has similar properties. Rice for Indian curries and pilafs should be fluffy and relatively dry; a long-grain rice is best for these dishes. Try basmati rice if you can find it and afford it. It has an intoxicating fragrance and a wonderful, slightly nutty flavor.

Shanta Nimbark Sacharoff, author of a fine Hindu cookbook, *The Flavors of India*, recommends converted rice as the best white rice for general use. Converted rice is parboiled and then steamed, which transports nutrients from the outer rice bran into the center of the grain. The result is fluffy, white, nearly foolproof rice with at least some of the nutritional value of brown rice. (Do not confuse converted rice with instant rice, which no one recommends.)

I generally keep two types of rice on hand—a medium or long-grain white rice and brown Texmati rice. The latter is a cross between basmati and American long-grain rice; it's expensive, but unlike other varieties of brown rice, it cooks quickly and my family will eat it.

SOY SAUCE

Good quality soy sauce is especially important in Japanese pickles and other strongly flavored dishes. Buy brands that are naturally fermented; they will say so on the label. Kikkoman is OK; tamari, which I buy in bulk at the food co-op, is better, having richer flavor and relatively low salt content. Some manufacturers add enzymes to shorten the fermentation process, and you don't have to be a connoisseur to notice the difference in taste that results.

SOUPS

BORSCHT

My friend Kristin Skotheim first served me this delicious vegetarian borscht, which she makes by the gallon from her garden and then freezes. It contains no cabbage, and the taste is fresh and bright. Don't be put off by the ketchup; many traditional borscht recipes call for tomato purée, sugar, and vinegar, which add up to ketchup anyway. You could substitute chili sauce for extra zip.

3 tablespoons oil

1 medium onion, diced

3 or 4 carrots, grated

4 large beets, peeled and grated

one 15-ounce can tomatoes, roughly chopped, with liquid

4 cups vegetable stock or water

½ cup ketchup

salt and pepper

2 tablespoons lemon juice

1 tablespoon fresh dill or 1 teaspoon dried

sour cream for garnish (optional)

Heat oil in a big soup kettle. Add onion and sauté until soft. Add carrots and beets and sauté another 5 minutes. Add tomatoes, stock or water, ketchup, salt, and pepper. Bring to a boil, lower heat to simmer, and cook, covered, until vegetables are tender, about 40 minutes. Stir in lemon juice and serve hot, sprinkled with dill. Garnish with a spoonful of sour cream if you like.

SERVES 6 AS A FIRST COURSE OR 4 AS A MAIN DISH.

HOT AND SOUR SHCHI

Russia runs on cabbage, and shchi *—a sauerkraut soup—is basic fare in its many variations. Because I find the traditional versions I've had a bit bland, I add red pepper flakes and vinegar to mine. If you have kim chee (page 167), you can substitute half a cup for half a cup of the kraut, and eliminate the pepper and vinegar. Shchi is traditionally served with boiled potatoes and sour cream.*

4 tablespoons butter or oil

1 medium onion, diced

1 medium stalk celery, diced

½ cup parsley, chopped

1 teaspoon red pepper flakes

1 pint sauerkraut, drained and washed

½ pound lean stew meat or chuck steak, sliced in ½-inch cubes and seared briefly, or 1 cup meat from the soup bones used to make the stock

5 cups beef stock

bouquet garni

salt and pepper

3 tablespoons cider vinegar

dill weed

Melt butter or oil in saucepan. Sauté onion, celery, parsley, red pepper flakes, and sauerkraut over low heat until kraut is golden. Add beef and stock, bouquet garni, salt, and pepper. Simmer for 2 hours. Add vinegar, simmer 2 minutes, sprinkle with dill weed, and serve hot.

SERVES 4 TO 6.

BROCCOLI YOGURT SOUP

I think this is better than cream of broccoli soup. The cilantro may seem like a lot, but the flavor moderates in cooking so it isn't overpowering. Hamburg parsley, if available, is a more conveniently sized root than celeriac for a half-cup quantity.

1 medium bunch broccoli

3 tablespoons butter

1 medium onion, coarsely chopped

½ cup chopped celeriac or Hamburg parsley

4 cups chicken broth

2 medium potatoes, peeled and cubed

salt and pepper

3 tablespoons chopped cilantro, divided

1 cup plain yogurt

1 cup milk or half-and-half

Separate broccoli into florets. Peel stalks and cut into 1-inch lengths.

Melt butter in large saucepan. Add onion and celeriac or Hamburg parsley and toss to coat. Stir over medium heat until onion is tender. Pour in chicken broth. Add broccoli, potatoes, salt, pepper, and 2 tablespoons of the chopped cilantro. Simmer covered for 20 minutes or until broccoli is tender.

Purée mixture and return to saucepan. In a separate bowl, mix together yogurt and milk or half-and-half, and add to soup. Warm gently, sprinkle with the remaining tablespoon of cilantro, and serve hot.

SERVES 6.

GARBURE

Garbures abound, and a really authentic one, like your mom's favorite spaghetti sauce, is unlikely to have a written recipe. Its common denominators are beans, cabbage, carrots, and leeks, and some portion of a pig, whether sausage or bacon or salt pork or ham hocks. The dish is indigenous to the Pyrenees, claimed both by the Basques and the Béarn region of France. It can be made a day or two ahead. I cannot vouch for the authenticity of this version, but it is easy, economical, and good. I cooked it the night before a ski trip and then reheated it when we returned home cold and hungry. Elizabeth David recommends adding a few whole roasted chestnuts along with the cabbage.

1/4 pound salt pork, chopped

1 medium onion, chopped

2 medium potatoes, peeled and chopped

2 leeks, chopped, with some green

1 rutabaga or turnip, peeled and chopped

1 large carrot, peeled and chopped

1 quart water

half a green cabbage, sliced thin

3 cloves garlic, crushed

1 bay leaf

2 cups cooked white beans or favas, drained

salt and pepper

1/2 pound garlic sausage, sliced

1 sprig fresh thyme or 1/4 teaspoon dried

2 tablespoons chopped parsley

Render salt pork in large, heavy soup kettle. Add onion and sauté until soft. Add potatoes, leeks, rutabaga or turnip, and carrot and sauté another 2 or 3 minutes. Add water, cabbage, garlic, bay leaf, beans, salt, and pepper and bring to a boil. Lower heat and simmer about an hour or until vegetables are tender. Add sausage, thyme, and parsley and cook another 10 minutes.

SERVES 6.

BASQUE SOUP

This is adapted from Elizabeth David's book of Mediterranean food, a great sourcebook of traditional recipes (with traditionally vague measurements). You may substitute olive oil for the lard; it won't taste the same, but it will be good. This soup has a robust flavor, as you'd expect, and with good bread and a salad, it makes a complete meal.

¼ cup lard or olive oil

1 medium onion, chopped

½ pound pumpkin, peeled and cubed

1 medium cabbage, sliced

½ pound dried haricot beans or navy beans, soaked overnight and drained

2 cloves garlic, sliced

2 quarts stock or water

salt and pepper

Heat lard or olive oil in a large, heavy saucepan or soup pot. Add onion and brown. Add pumpkin, cabbage, beans, and garlic and cook briefly, stirring to coat the vegetables with oil.

Add stock or water, salt, and pepper, and bring to a boil. Lower heat to simmer and cook gently, covered, until beans are tender, about 2 hours. Adjust seasoning before serving.

SERVES 6.

CARIBBEAN CABBAGE SOUP

This soup must be served good and hot. And don't overcook the cabbage. Apart from these two points, it's foolproof. You can use cooked shrimp instead of fresh; add them just before serving and heat through.

2 tablespoons light oil

1 teaspoon chopped fresh ginger

3 tablespoons minced onion

2 cups shredded green cabbage

6 cups water

1½ cups diced unpeeled potatoes

½ pound raw shrimp, shelled and coarsely chopped (tiny shrimp can be used whole)

salt and pepper

hot pepper sauce

1 tablespoon lemon juice

chives

Heat oil in a heavy saucepan or skillet. Add ginger and onion and sauté briefly. Add cabbage and sauté, stirring, until limp, about 3 minutes.

Bring water to a boil in a large kettle. Add potatoes and the cabbage mixture and simmer until potatoes are tender, about 15 minutes.

Add shrimp, salt, pepper, and a dash of hot pepper sauce and simmer another 5 minutes. Remove from heat and add lemon juice. Serve immediately, garnished with chopped chives.

SERVES 4.

CELERIAC SOUP

This soup is from Bruce Naftaly, co-proprietor of Le Gourmand in Seattle. In the words of its creator, "It sounds rather homely, but it's wonderful." Jerusalem artichokes can be substituted for the celeriac.

4 medium celeriacs

2½ cups veal, chicken, or vegetable stock

salt and white pepper

½ cup whipping cream (optional)

Peel celeriacs and cut into small pieces. Hold the cut pieces in acidulated water. Drain celeriac and put in a saucepan with stock to cover, about 2 cups. Simmer until soft, about 30 minutes. Remove from heat, purée, and return to pan. Add salt and freshly ground white pepper to taste. Thin if desired with more stock or whipping cream.

SERVES 4.

CHESTNUT SOUP

This recipe is from John Doerper, whose books and magazine columns sing the praises and chastise the shortcomings of Northwest kitchens. The ginger saves the dish from overpowering richness. Doerper uses whipping cream and tops each serving with a spoonful of salmon caviar. I can't handle that much high living.

1 pound fresh chestnuts

¼ cup butter

6 to 8 shallots, minced, or 1 small yellow onion, chopped

½ cup celeriac, chopped fine

2 cups chicken stock

salt and white pepper

⅛ teaspoon nutmeg

1 cup half-and-half

chopped parsley

pickled ginger (available in Asian markets)

Cut a slash on the flat side of each chestnut shell. Simmer until they are quite soft, about 15 minutes. Remove nuts from water, shell, and remove brown skins with a sharp knife.

Heat butter in a large saucepan. Sauté shallots or onion over medium heat until golden. Add chestnuts. Cook about a minute to coat outside of nuts and seal in flavors. Stir constantly to keep from burning.

Add celeriac and stir well. Add chicken stock. Bring to a boil, then cover and reduce heat. Simmer 20 to 30 minutes or until chestnuts are very tender. Strain chestnuts, shallot or onion, and celeriac from stock. Return stock to pan. Purée chestnuts and vegetables and return them to saucepan, stirring well. Bring mixture to a boil. Season with salt, white pepper, and nutmeg.

Add cream. Reheat but do not boil. Ladle into bowls. Garnish each bowl with chopped parsley and a slice of pickled ginger.

SERVES 4 TO 6.

SPICY CHESTNUT SOUP

This is a real departure from the mild, creamy soups usually made with chestnuts. It has a full, dark taste, enlivened with cayenne. Many gardeners make their own vegetable stock out of peels and trimmings. Commercial powdered stocks also work well, but you'll need to find one that's not too salty.

2 pounds fresh chestnuts or 1 pound canned unsweetened chestnut purée

1 quart vegetable stock

1 cup finely grated carrot or salsify

2 tablespoons butter

2 tablespoons flour

½ cup red wine

¼ teaspoon nutmeg

¼ teaspoon cayenne

salt and pepper

paprika

finely chopped parsley

If chestnuts are fresh, cut an X in each one and then simmer in water to cover for 15 minutes or roast in the oven 15 to 20 minutes at 375°F. Peel chestnuts and purée, adding a bit of the vegetable stock if necessary. Add purée and grated carrot or salsify to remaining stock and simmer slowly for about 30 minutes.

Melt butter in another pot. Sprinkle in flour and cook, stirring, until roux begins to color. Add hot soup slowly to roux, whisking to keep it well blended. Add wine, nutmeg, cayenne, salt, and pepper, and simmer another 10 minutes over very low heat, stirring often.

Sprinkle a little paprika and parsley over each serving.

SERVES 6.

ITALIAN GREENS AND RICE SOUP

The slight bitterness of cooked escarole or chicory is just right with the mild flavors of chicken and rice. A great, simple soup.

1 pound escarole or chicory

3 tablespoons olive oil

2 teaspoons finely chopped garlic

1 small onion, chopped

salt

5 cups chicken broth

½ cup long-grain rice

black pepper

Parmesan cheese

Separate all the leaves of the escarole or chicory. Soak briefly in basin of water, drain, and cut crosswise into pieces about 1 inch wide.

Heat olive oil in heavy soup kettle and sauté garlic and onion until onion is pale gold, about 3 minutes. Add escarole or chicory, sprinkle lightly with salt, and cook 3 minutes more. Add 1 cup of broth, cover, and cook over low heat until escarole is quite tender, 10 to 15 minutes.

Add rest of broth and bring to boil. Add rice, cover, and simmer about 12 minutes or until rice is tender but firm to the bite. Taste and correct seasonings; add several grinds of black pepper.

Sprinkle with Parmesan cheese just before serving.

SERVES 4.

FENNEL AND SHALLOT SOUP

Shallots are a vegetable luxury that you can indulge in in quantity if you have any garden space at all. The pinkish-brown bulbs are easy to grow and extremely hardy, and the foliage is decorative (or at least unobtrusive) enough to combine with ornamentals. I grow shallots, columbine, eggplant, and larkspur in a sunny strip next to my house. The effect might not be to everyone's taste, but I think it's gorgeous, both in the yard and in the kitchen. Little yellow multiplier onions are sometimes sold as shallots. Hold out for the real thing.

1 tablespoon butter

1 cup shallots, peeled and chopped

2 cups poultry stock

2 pounds fennel (about 2 large bulbs), trimmed, cored, and sliced

1 tablespoon fennel seeds

½ cup half-and-half

½ cup sour cream

salt and pepper

¼ cup minced fennel tops

2 tablespoons grated Parmesan cheese (optional)

Melt butter in large, heavy saucepan over low heat. Add shallots and cook, stirring often, about 10 minutes or until they begin to soften. Add stock, fennel bulbs, and fennel seeds. Simmer until fennel is very tender, about 30 minutes, stirring occasionally. (Soup can be made ahead up to this point and refrigerated for a day or two.)

Press soup through a sieve, return to saucepan, and bring to a simmer. Whisk in half-and-half and sour cream. Season with salt and pepper. Add fennel tops. Ladle soup into bowls. Garnish with Parmesan cheese if desired.

SERVES 4.

GREEN SOUP

Versions of this soup appear in a number of books, credited to the sudden inspiration of gardeners on both sides of the Atlantic. It also bears a resemblance to the 18th-century recipe for Potage Parmentier. Some recipes call for a combination of spinach and sorrel, or you could replace the sorrel with watercress or arugula. Because the greens are barely cooked, this is not the place for tough customers like collards and chard.

3 tablespoons butter

half a medium onion, chopped

2 medium potatoes, peeled and diced

1 quart chicken stock

salt and pepper

2 cups sorrel leaves or a combination of greens

2 tablespoons dry sherry

$\frac{1}{2}$ cup cream

fresh nutmeg

chopped parsley

chopped chives

Melt butter in a heavy saucepan and cook onion until soft but not brown. Add potatoes and cover with stock. Season with salt and pepper and simmer until potatoes are tender, about 15 minutes.

Pour a cup of soup and a handful of greens into the blender and purée at high speed. Repeat until all the soup and greens are blended. The mixture should be a nice, fresh green.

Return mixture to saucepan, add sherry, and reheat. Add a little more stock or water if soup is very thick. Stir in cream, heat, and correct seasoning. Add several grinds of fresh nutmeg.

Serve hot, garnished with parsley and chives.

SERVES 6.

INNISFREE JERUSALEM ARTICHOKE SOUP

My friends Fred and Lynn Berman specialize in fresh seasonal food at Innisfree, their restaurant in Glacier, Washington. Much of it is grown on their own farm, and patrons can stroll through the woods to their garden a few hundred yards away.

4 tablespoons butter or oil

2 leeks, sliced lengthwise and cut into half-rounds

3 celery stalks, diced

1 small fennel bulb, diced

1 teaspoon chopped parsley

1 teaspoon fresh or dried dill weed

salt and pepper

2 to 3 pounds Jerusalem artichokes, scrubbed and coarsely chopped

2 large potatoes, scrubbed and diced

2 quarts chicken or vegetable stock

1 cup half-and-half or nonfat yogurt

fennel leaves, for garnish

Melt butter or oil in medium soup pot. Add leeks, celery, and fennel and sauté until vegetables are just beginning to soften, 3 or 4 minutes. Add parsley, dill, salt, and pepper. Stir. Add Jerusalem artichokes, potatoes, and stock and bring to a simmer. Cook until artichokes are just tender, 15 to 20 minutes. Remove from heat. Purée about two-thirds of soup and return to pot. Add half-and-half or yogurt, stir, and heat through. Serve in heated bowls, garnished with fennel.

SERVES 4 TO 6.

JERUSALEM ARTICHOKE SOUP PROVENÇALE
(POTAGE DE TOPINAMBOURS À LA PROVENÇALE)

Jerusalem artichokes go well with a little ham or bacon. The flavor is similar to that of a traditional ham and bean soup, but this soup is much lighter. It's also one of the fastest soups because Jerusalem artichokes cook very quickly.

2 pounds Jerusalem artichokes, scrubbed and diced

6 cups water

salt

1 cup milk

2 tablespoons olive oil

½ cup drained canned tomatoes

1 clove garlic, crushed

1 tablespoon chopped parsley

2 tablespoons chopped ham or bacon (optional)

Bring salted water to boil, add artichokes, lower heat, and cook until tender. Purée and return to heat. Add milk gradually and heat slowly. Heat olive oil in a small skillet; add tomatoes, garlic, parsley, and ham or bacon (if used). Cook briefly, no more than 2 minutes, and then pour mixture into artichoke purée. Heat to just below boiling and serve hot.

SERVES 6.

BROSE

The British food writer Jane Grigson includes this heirloom Scottish soup in the roster of "Good Things" (in the book of the same title). Her description gives the flavor of a time, gone for most of us, when the homestead's produce meant the difference between want and plenty:

> A simple soup made by cooking various items, or one item, in water and thickening it eventually with a handful of lightly-toasted oatmeal.
>
> Kail brose, flavored with curly kale, is the most famous. By extension, the word kail covers all vegetables and even all food. An invitation to kail means to dinner.
>
> This recipe uses beef and would have been considered a luxury meal for a poor household, especially if the bones contained marrow. Grigson scorns precise ingredient measurements as not only superfluous but misleading, so the amounts and temperatures given here are mine.

1 pound beef soup bones

3 quarts water

2 cups shredded kale

½ cup rolled oats

salt and pepper

Bring water to a boil in a large kettle, add soup bones, and simmer for 2 to 3 hours, skimming as necessary. Strain soup, saving bones, return to pot, and skim off fat. Add kale and cook about 15 minutes.

Meanwhile, heat oven to 250°F. Toast rolled oats on a baking sheet until they are crumbly but not brown, about 20 minutes. Put oats into a bowl, stir in a ladleful of soup, and return mixture to soup pot. Simmer, stirring, until slightly thickened.

Remove meat from soup bones, shred, and return to pot. Season to taste.

Nettles, scallions, or leeks can be substituted for kale.

SERVES 6.

CALDO VERDE

This is Portugal's best-known soup, and it also marks one of the first uses of the potato in European cooking. When times were hard and the household sausage supply was gone, families poured the soup over crusty slices of bread. Vegetarians can use the same method today, increasing the amount of garlic to compensate for the missing sausage spices. Flavor counts more than texture here, so it's a good place to use weatherbeaten kale or collards. Some recipes tell you to purée the cooked potatoes. I prefer them simply diced.

3 tablespoons olive oil

1 or more cloves garlic

1 medium leek with 2 inches green, chopped

2 medium potatoes, scrubbed and and diced

1 linguiça, chorizo, or other spicy sausage, sliced

5 cups chicken or vegetable stock

1 pound kale or collards (one large bunch), shredded, with tough ribs removed

salt and pepper

Heat olive oil in soup kettle, add garlic and leek, and sauté gently until leek becomes transparent. Add potatoes, sausage, and stock, bring to boil, and simmer until potatoes are tender, about 10 minutes. Add shredded kale or collards and cook another 5 to 10 minutes, depending on toughness of kale. Add salt and pepper to taste and serve hot.

SERVES 6.

SOUPE BONNE FEMME

Louis Diat, the creator of vichyssoise, said his family used to have this hot potato-leek soup for breakfast. If you want to follow his example, you could do the simmering the night before and add the hot milk in the morning. (Vichyssoise-loving gardeners can ensure a summer supply by making potato-leek pureé in quantity, just before their leeks bolt to seed. It freezes well. When hot weather comes, just thaw the purée and complete your favorite recipe.)

2 large or 4 medium leeks

3 tablespoons butter

½ cup coarsely chopped onion

2 medium potatoes, diced

salt

3 cups boiling water

2 cups hot milk

chopped parsley or chives

Cut leeks in half lengthwise and then dice crosswise into ½-inch pieces. Wash and dry.

Melt 2 tablespoons of butter in a heavy saucepan, add leeks and onion, and cook over low heat, covered, until translucent, about 5 minutes. Stir frequently and don't let them brown. Add potatoes, salt, and boiling water. Bring to boil, cover, and simmer 25 minutes.

Add hot milk and remaining butter and serve hot, sprinkled with parsley or chives.

SERVES 4.

MUSHROOM SOUP

My mother makes the best mushroom soup in the world. This is our best attempt to quantify what she does by intuition and improvisation. The original recipe, long lost, came from her friend Myrtle James. The soup contains no milk or cream, so the mushroom flavor is intensified. If you are a mushroom gatherer, this is a great showcase for your favorite flavors.

2 tablespoons butter or margarine

2 tablespoons oil

1 clove garlic, minced

1 to 2 pounds fresh mushrooms, quartered if small, sliced if large

salt and pepper

$\frac{1}{4}$ cup dry sherry

$\frac{1}{2}$ teaspoon dried basil

$\frac{1}{2}$ cup chopped green onions or chives

2 tablespoons chopped parsley

6 cups chicken stock

freshly grated nutmeg

CREAM OF NETTLE SOUP

Revenge is one motive for eating nettles, but there are others. The stinging plant is one of the earliest greens up in the spring, and it is very nutritious. Nettle dishes, especially soups, are traditional in French, Scottish, and Welsh cooking. Always wear gloves for gathering and cleaning. Rubber dish gloves are good. Surgeon's gloves might be even better.

4 cups young nettle leaves

2 cups chicken or vegetable stock

2 cups milk or light cream

2 tablespoons grated onion

2 tablespoons butter

2 tablespoons flour

salt and pepper

Parmesan cheese

Wash nettles and steam until soft in the water that clings to them. Purée with their liquid, adding some stock by the tablespoon if necessary. Melt butter in a medium saucepan, add onion, and cook until soft. Add flour and cook, stirring constantly, until color starts to turn. Add stock, salt, pepper, and nettle purée and heat to boiling. Lower heat and simmer 10 minutes. Add milk or cream and heat gently. Sprinkle each serving with Parmesan cheese to taste.

SERVES 4.

PARSNIP STEW

Jerusalem artichokes can be substituted for the parsnips. You could also use fish stock in place of the water and add a few oysters along with the spinach. The sweet roots and rich spinach taste make a wonderful, earthy combination.

¼ pound (4 strips) lean bacon, cut into small pieces

1 medium onion, chopped

4 medium parsnips, scrubbed and diced

3 medium potatoes, scrubbed and diced

2 cups boiling water

4 cups milk, scalded

1 cup spinach leaves, chopped fine

3 tablespoons melted butter

3 tablespoons flour

salt and pepper

dill weed, fresh or dried

Cook bacon in a heavy pot or flameproof casserole until it begins to crisp. Remove bacon from pan, drain, and reserve.

Sauté onion in bacon fat until golden. Add parsnips and potatoes, stirring to coat them well. Cook, stirring, about 5 minutes over medium heat. Add boiling water, lower heat, and simmer, covered, until roots are tender, about 20 minutes. Add milk and spinach and heat through.

Blend butter and flour in a small mixing bowl. Stir a cup of soup into the butter mixture. Pour it back into the pot and simmer, stirring constantly, until soup is thickened and smooth. Season to taste with salt and pepper. Stir in bacon and sprinkle with dill.

SERVES 6.

TWO-PUMPKIN SOUP

A lot of pumpkin soups feature sweet spices and lots of cream, and in truth they rather resemble pumpkin pie. I prefer savory spices with pumpkin and squash, such as this soup from Le Gourmand in Seattle, which is flavored with juniper berries. Bruce Naftaly makes it with pie pumpkin and Japanese Hokkaido squash, a sweet-fleshed variety related to the North American Hubbard. You can substitute your favorite squash for one or both varieties. Bruce sautés the vegetables in goose fat, but good results can be obtained with other fats or oils.

2 tablespoons rendered goose fat, home-rendered lard, butter, or olive oil

1 medium leek, white part only, chopped

1 medium onion, chopped

¾ cup pie pumpkin, peeled and diced

¾ cup Hokkaido squash, peeled and diced

1 teaspoon ground juniper berries

2 cups white stock, made with veal, chicken, or vegetables

⅛ teaspoon white pepper

salt to taste

Heat fat or oil in a saucepan. Add leek and onion and sauté until soft. Add pumpkin, squash, and juniper berries and cook gently, stirring occasionally, for about 10 minutes. Add stock and simmer for about 30 minutes or until pumpkin and squash are soft. Remove from heat, purée, and return to pan. Thin as needed with more stock. Add pepper and salt to taste.

SERVES 4.

Root Vegetable and Leek Soup
with Gouda Cheese

This rustic soup is a perfect marriage of form and content. It uses plain winter ingredients to provide the comfort and uplift we need on gray days. The recipe is from Ron Zimmerman, chef at The Herbfarm restaurant in the Cascade foothills east of Seattle. Zimmerman uses Yakima Valley Gouda. I like Pleasant Valley Gouda, which is made near my home in Whatcom County. The point in this recipe is not to worry about brand names but to pay the price for a good-quality cheese. If your experience with Gouda is limited to those rubbery little hockey pucks that get passed around at Christmastime, you'll be amazed at how good it can be.

2 tablespoons butter

1 small onion, chopped

3 leeks, white and pale green parts, washed well and chopped fine

3 cups strong chicken stock

1 salsify root (or small amount of turnip or parsnip), peeled and grated

6 medium potatoes, peeled and chopped

salt and pepper

1 carrot, grated

2 cups milk

1 cup shredded Gouda cheese

chives (optional)

carrot rounds, cut into stars (optional)

Melt butter in large saucepan or soup pot. Add onion, leeks, and a little salt and sauté over medium heat, stirring, until soft, about 15 minutes. Don't rush this part—proper slow cooking brings out a certain natural sweetness.

Add chicken stock and salsify and heat to simmering. Add potatoes. Cover without stirring (you want the potatoes to stay on top) and cook until potatoes are tender, about 25 minutes. Lift out potatoes with a slotted spoon, purée, and return to soup. Add a little salt and a generous amount of pepper. Bring soup to a boil, add carrots, and stir in milk. Bring just to boiling, add cheese, adjust seasoning, and heat through. Do not boil again.

Serve in shallow bowls, sprinkled with chives and a few floated carrot stars, if used.

SERVES 6 AS A SOUP COURSE
OR 3 AS A MAIN COURSE.

CHEESE AND LEEK SOUP

You need a bone-dry wine and a good quality Swiss or Gruyère to make this work. Otherwise, skip the wine and cheese and stick with a good, simple leek and rice soup.

6 leeks, rinsed and sliced, with the tender green part

⅓ cup rice

6 cups beef stock

salt and pepper

1½ cups Swiss or Gruyère cheese, grated

1½ cups dry white wine

In a large saucepan, combine leeks, rice, and beef stock. Bring to a boil, reduce heat, and simmer for 20 minutes or until leeks and rice are done. Season to taste with salt and pepper.

Combine cheese and wine in top of a double boiler. Hold over simmering water until cheese is melted and stir until smooth. Spoon cheese and wine mixture into individual soup bowls, ladle boiling soup over the top, and serve.

SERVES 4 TO 6.

WINTER-RUN SOUP

This was inspired by a Nooksack River steelhead and my January garden. It has a wonderful, delicate flavor.

Stock

bones and trimmings, including head and tail, of a salmon or steelhead

2 stalks celery, with leaves

1 medium onion, quartered

4 cups water

1 cup white wine

salt and pepper to taste

Combine all ingredients and cook gently for 45 minutes, strain, and refrigerate if not to be used immediately.

Soup

$^1/_2$ cup olive oil, divided

2 cups Jerusalem artichokes, scrubbed and cubed

1 cup celeriac, peeled and cubed, or 2 stalks diced celery

5 cups salmon or vegetable stock

1 large leek, with some green, cut in 1-inch sections

2 cups salmon or steelhead, in 1-inch pieces

1 teaspoon dried basil

1 teaspoon fresh tarragon or $^1/_2$ teaspoon dried

salt and pepper

2 tablespoons flour

1$^1/_2$ cups half-and-half

Heat ¼ cup of the oil in a medium skillet and sauté Jerusalem artichokes and celeriac for about 5 minutes over medium-low heat. They should not be cooked through. Bring stock to a boil in a soup pot, add artichokes and celeriac, and simmer about 10 minutes.

Meanwhile, sauté leeks and fish briefly in the remaining ¼ cup oil. Add to stock with basil, tarragon, salt, and pepper, and cook gently another 10 minutes or until celeriac is tender.

Put flour in small bowl. Slowly pour in ½ cup of stock, stirring constantly. Return mixture to soup, stirring to blend evenly. Add half-and-half and reheat soup. Stir until soup thickens slightly but don't let it boil.

SERVES 6 AS A SOUP COURSE OR 3 AS A MAIN COURSE.

FISH SOUP FROM FUJIAN

This is so easy. You can walk in the door at 7 and have it on the table at 7:20. It's good with Chinese cabbage as well as bok choy, and I've even made it with romaine in a pinch. The rich, strong tamari soy sauce I usually favor is too strong here, overpowering the fish. If you must use it, cut back to 1 tablespoon.

½ pound firm fish fillet

1½ tablespoons light soy sauce

¼ teaspoon red pepper flakes

1 teaspoon cornstarch

½ teaspoon salt

1 tablespoon sesame oil

1 quart chicken stock

2 big slices fresh ginger

2 cups thinly sliced bok choy

Slice fish into ¼-inch strips. Blend soy sauce, red pepper flakes, cornstarch, salt, and sesame oil. Toss with fish strips and let stand 15 minutes.

Bring stock to a boil. Add fresh ginger and bok choy. Lower heat to simmer for 5 minutes. Gently add fish mixture and stir carefully. Cover and simmer 5 minutes.

SERVES 4.

SPINACH SOUP WITH GRAIN DUMPLINGS

I'm very fond of this unusual soup, which combines a hearty dumpling with a fresh vegetable taste.

4 tablespoons butter

2 cups minced onion

2 quarts beef or vegetable stock

1½ cups rolled oats

½ cup bulgur

1 teaspoon salt

¼ teaspoon pepper

½ cup warm water

2 tablespoons tomato paste

1 tablespoon fresh lemon juice

1 pound fresh spinach (1 big bunch), chopped fine

Melt butter in large soup kettle and sauté onion until translucent. Add stock and bring to a boil. In a mixing bowl combine rolled oats, bulgur, salt, and pepper. Add warm water and mix with fingers until batter is stiff. It will be sticky. Form into balls no more than 1 inch in diameter and drop into hot soup. Cover and simmer 20 minutes. Mix together tomato paste and lemon juice and add to soup along with spinach. Cover and simmer 3 to 5 minutes. Serve hot.

SERVES 6.

SALADS

CORN SALAD AND ARUGULA WITH BEETS

This is a gardener's salad, reprinted from the Nichols Garden Nursery catalog. It combines two of my favorite winter greens with beets.

4 cups mixed corn salad and arugula

1 cup sliced cooked beets

2 chopped green onions or very small leeks

¼ cup olive oil

3 tablespoons red wine vinegar

1 teaspoon Dijon mustard

salt and pepper

Wash greens, place in a bowl, and arrange beets and onions on top. Dress with oil, vinegar, mustard, and salt and pepper to taste.

SERVES 4.

BEET SALAD WITH GARLIC SAUCE

This is a good, simple salad, even without the pungent skordalia.

1 pound beets

3 tablespoons light-flavored olive oil

2 tablespoons red wine vinegar

½ small onion, sliced thin

1 cup skordalia (see page 216)

Simmer beets in 2 cups water until tender. Drain, reserving 2 tablespoons of the cooking liquid. When beets are cool enough to handle, peel, slice thin, and arrange in a serving bowl with onion slices.

Combine oil, vinegar, and cooking liquid, pour over vegetables, and mix well. Serve chilled, with skordalia.

SERVES 4 TO 6.

RUSSIAN BEET SALAD

You don't have to already be a beet fan to like this, although you must appreciate garlic. The deep red beets and neon-pink mayonnaise make a vivid—not to say alarming—combination.

1 pound beets

2 cloves garlic, minced

⅓ cup chopped walnuts

¼ cup chopped prunes (soak prunes for 20 minutes in hot water if they are getting hard)

3 tablespoons mayonnaise

salt and pepper

Scrub beets and remove green tops. Bake at 375°F until soft, up to 2 hours, or in a microwave oven for 15 minutes. When they are cool enough to handle, slip off the skins and shred coarsely.

Combine beets with garlic, walnuts, and prunes. Add mayonnaise and mix well. Season to taste with salt and pepper and chill well before serving.

SERVES 6.

BRUSSELS SPROUT SALAD

This salad needs small, sweet Brussels sprouts. Gardeners have an immense advantage here, for although Brussels sprouts keep fairly well, they hold their peak of flavor only briefly.

3 tablespoons fresh lemon juice, divided

1½ cups sliced Jerusalem artichokes

1 large celeriac, peeled and sliced into bite-sized pieces (discard any corky center portion)

4 small leeks (white part only), chopped

1 pound fresh Brussels sprouts

3 tablespoons olive oil

1 tablespoon fresh grated lemon rind (optional)

salt and pepper

2 tablespoons chopped parsley

Combine 1 tablespoon of the lemon juice and 3 cups of water in a medium bowl. Add Jerusalem artichoke and celeriac slices and let stand, covered, in refrigerator until it's time to dress the salad.

Cook leeks in an inch of boiling, salted water until tender but not slimy, about 5 minutes. Drain, saving the water. Bring water back to a boil and steam Brussels sprouts only until crisp-tender, about 8 to 10 minutes.

Put leeks and Brussels sprouts in a serving bowl. Drain Jerusalem artichoke and celeriac well and add. Dress with olive oil, the remaining 2 tablespoons of lemon juice, and lemon rind (if used). Add salt and pepper to taste, mix, and check for seasoning.

Cover and let stand in refrigerator for an hour before serving. Garnish with chopped parsley.

SERVES 4.

ANTIBES COLESLAW

I don't like regular coleslaw, but I love this.

1 small cabbage

1 garlic clove, crushed

6 tablespoons olive oil

2½ tablespoons red or white wine vinegar

3 or 4 anchovy fillets, packed in oil, drained and minced

1 teaspoon Dijon mustard

salt and pepper

Wash cabbage, remove outer leaves, cut in half, and remove core. Slice thin. Combine remaining ingredients in small bowl, mix well, and blend with cabbage. Allow to stand for 10 minutes and serve.

SERVES 6.

ESCAROLE AND CABBAGE SALAD

This beautiful, robust salad will round off a meal of soup or burgers.

2 cups shredded escarole

2 cups shredded red cabbage

4 green onions or small leeks

4 tablespoons olive oil

2 tablespoons red wine vinegar or raspberry vinegar

2 teaspoons Dijon mustard

salt and pepper

Combine escarole and red cabbage in a bowl. Combine olive oil, vinegar, mustard, salt, and pepper and pour over greens.

SERVES 4.

CABBAGE SALAD WITH RASPBERRY VINEGAR

Workers at Alm Hill Gardens in Whatcom County get a fringe benefit in the form of Gretchen Hoyt's cooking. Alm Hill's raspberry vinegar is exceptionally fruity, and Gretchen uses it in this unusual salad combination.

1 small green cabbage, sliced thin

4 green onions or very small leeks, chopped

½ cup raisins

⅓ cup chopped black olives

salt and pepper

½ cup mayonnaise

¼ cup raspberry vinegar

Stir cabbage, green onions or leeks, raisins, and black olives together in a salad bowl. Sprinkle with salt and pepper to taste. Combine mayonnaise and raspberry vinegar and pour over salad. Toss and serve immediately.

SERVES 6 TO 8.

CARROT SALADS

The first summer carrots are so sweet and crisp and beautiful that it would be counterproductive to do anything more than scrub them. By midwinter, however, my garden holdovers need some help to look as good as they taste. The quality of grocery carrots—always variable—gets more so as storage time lengthens. This is the time for marinades. Here are three good ones:

Marinated Cooked Carrots

This is from the British food writer Elizabeth David. Cooking the carrots briefly in the marinade gives them an intense flavor. They still should have a bit of crunch.

½ cup water

½ cup white wine vinegar

½ cup white wine or dry sherry

½ cup olive oil

1 tablespoon parsley, chopped

1 teaspoon fresh thyme

1 teaspoon salt

1 clove garlic

pinch cayenne

1 pound carrots (about 6 medium), scrubbed and quartered

½ teaspoon smooth Dijon mustard

Bring to a boil all but the last two ingredients. Add carrots and cook, uncovered, at medium-high heat until they are barely tender. Drain carrots, reserving liquid. Arrange carrots in a serving bowl. Add mustard to liquid, mix well, and pour over carrots. Cool for at least an hour before serving.

SERVES 6.

Moroccan Carrot Salad

1 pound carrots (about 6 medium), scrubbed

2 shallots, chopped fine

2 to 3 tablespoons sugar

½ teaspoon salt

½ teaspoon ground cumin

pepper

dash cayenne

3 tablespoons lemon juice

½ cup finely minced parsley

Grate or julienne carrots. Add shallots and toss. Combine sugar, salt, and cumin and toss with carrots. Season with pepper and cayenne. Add lemon juice and toss again. Marinate for 1 hour. Sprinkle with parsley and serve at room temperature.

SERVES 6.

Italian Carrot Marinade

This traditional treatment is from Marcella Hazan's Classic Italian Cookbook. *You have to make it at least a day in advance. Tarragon can replace the oregano for a change in flavor.*

4 medium carrots, scrubbed

1 clove garlic, lightly crushed

1 teaspoon fresh oregano or 1/4 teaspoon dried

salt and pepper

1 tablespoon red wine vinegar

olive oil

Cut carrots into 2-inch lengths and steam until barely tender. Drain and cut lengthwise into matchsticks. Place in small, deep serving dish and bury garlic in carrots. Add oregano, salt and pepper, vinegar, and enough olive oil to cover. Marinate, refrigerated, overnight or longer. Remove garlic after 24 hours. Serve at room temperature.

SERVES 3 TO 4.

COOKED CELERIAC SALAD

I first saw this recipe in a Russian cookbook, but I think it must date from the time when French cooking was mandatory at socially correct tables. The cooking liquid, with its subtle celery flavor, makes a superior stock.

2 cups chicken stock

3 tablespoons chopped onion

1/2 teaspoon peppercorns

1 bay leaf

1 medium celeriac, peeled and cut in half

1/4 cup olive oil

1/4 cup white wine vinegar

1 teaspoon dry mustard

salt and pepper

1 tablespoon minced parsley

Put chicken stock, onion, peppercorns, and bay leaf in a saucepan. Bring to boil, add celeriac, and simmer until celeriac is barely tender. Remove celeriac. Strain stock and save for another use.

When celeriac is cool enough to handle, cut into 1/2-inch cubes. Make a dressing of olive oil, vinegar, and mustard and pour over warm celeriac. Add salt and pepper to taste, sprinkle with parsley, and toss. Let stand for an hour at room temperature, and then chill before serving.

SERVES 4.

CELERIAC AND BEET SALAD

Served hot, this also makes a nice side dish.

2 medium beets

1 medium celeriac

⅓ cup olive oil

salt and pepper

juice of 2 lemons

Boil or bake beets. Peel and julienne when cool enough to handle. Peel and slice celeriac and steam until just tender. Mix beets and celeriac. Make a dressing of olive oil, salt, pepper, and lemon juice. Pour over vegetables and chill before serving.

SERVES 4 TO 6.

CELERIAC AND SHRIMP WITH MUSTARD DRESSING

French cooks will recognize this as a jazzed-up version of Celeriac Rémoulade. Here, the celeriac is grated raw instead of julienned and blanched. Small roots are best for this dish. You could use crab in place of shrimp.

2 eggs

1 tablespoon Dijon mustard

2 teaspoons white wine vinegar

salt and pepper

¾ cup light oil

3 small celeriacs, peeled and coarsely grated

1 tablespoon lemon juice

12 cooked deveined shrimp, cubed

minced chives or green onions

Mix eggs, mustard, vinegar, salt, and pepper in blender or food processor for about 30 seconds. Begin adding oil by drops and continue blending until mixture is thick and smooth. Taste and adjust seasonings if necessary.

Sprinkle celeriac with a little lemon juice. Add dressing. Toss with shrimp and chives or green onions until well blended. Chill 3 to 4 hours before serving.

SERVES 6.

CELERIAC RÉMOULADE

A classic of French cooking, simple and satisfying.

half a lemon

1 or 2 celeriac roots (about 1 pound total)

2 tablespoons Dijon mustard

1 tablespoon red wine vinegar

salt and pepper

¼ cup light oil

2 tablespoons chopped parsley

Cut lemon into two wedges. Squeeze one wedge into a medium bowl of water and the other into a saucepan with a quart of water. Bring water in saucepan to a boil. Meanwhile, peel celeriac and cut into julienne slices. There should be 3 to 4 cups. Keep unsliced pieces in the lemon water, and return the julienned slices to the lemon water as you prepare them. Drain slices and blanch briefly in the boiling water. Drain again and dry on a towel.

Whisk mustard, vinegar, salt, and pepper together in a large bowl. Add about 2 tablespoons of oil, beating energetically, and then add the rest in droplets, whisking all the while. Fold celeriac into the sauce and marinate for several hours. Garnish with chopped parsley just before serving.

SERVES 4 TO 6.

ENDIVE AND WATERCRESS SALAD

If you grow your own endive, this high-ticket salad is suddenly affordable. Even if you don't, it's worth it once in a while.

4 heads endive, cored and cut into bite-sized pieces

1 large bunch watercress (leaves and small stems only)

1 small clove garlic, cut lengthwise

4 tablespoons olive oil

salt and pepper

2 tablespoons red wine vinegar

Rub salad bowl with garlic. Combine endive, cress, and olive oil in salad bowl and toss. Add salt, pepper, and vinegar and toss again.

SERVES 4.

FENNEL AND APPLE SALAD

 If you don't already like fennel, this probably won't change your mind, but if you do it's a nice fresh taste. My children like it better than Waldorf salad.

2 heads fennel, trimmed and chopped

4 medium apples, cored and chopped

2 tablespoons lemon juice

salt and pepper

¼ cup sunflower seeds

3 tablespoons oil

2 teaspoons sugar

watercress (optional)

Put fennel and apples in a bowl, sprinkle with lemon juice, and mix. Add salt, pepper, and sunflower seeds and mix again. Dissolve sugar in oil, pour over salad, and mix. Garnish with watercress if you like.

SERVES 6.

KOHLRABI SALAD

Small kohlrabi are best for salads.

4 small kohlrabi, peeled

salt

2 tablespoons soy sauce

½ teaspoon sugar

1 teaspoon hot pepper sauce

3 tablespoons toasted sesame oil

3 stalks celery, chopped, or 1 cup chopped celeriac

3 or 4 green onions, chopped

Grate kohlrabi, sprinkle with salt, and let stand for 30 minutes. Rinse and drain. Blend soy sauce, sugar, and hot pepper sauce. Gradually add sesame oil, whisking constantly. Add kohlrabi, celery or celeriac, and green onions, toss, and chill for at least 1 hour. Toss again before serving.

SERVES 4.

TIBETAN SALAD

Tibetans make this salad from buck-wheat greens, one of the very few leafy vegetables that can grow in their extreme climate. Gardeners who use buckwheat as a summer cover crop can experience the authentic taste. Buckwheat is not available in winter, but my friend Rinjing Dorje, author of Food in Tibetan Life, *whence this recipe comes, says a combination of spinach and watercress makes a good substitute. Fenugreek seeds are as hard as the rocks they resemble, but they soften when cooked. Incidentally, fenugreek is easy to grow in Northwest gardens, and the bitter greens can be used with discretion in salads. The Nichols catalog has seed, and sprouting fenugreek is available in some natural foods stores.*

1 bunch fresh spinach

1 bunch watercress

1 teaspoon honey

2 cloves garlic, crushed

1/2 teaspoon red pepper flakes

salt

1/4 cup hot water

1 cup yogurt

1 tablespoon vegetable oil

1/4 teaspoon fenugreek seeds

Remove stems from greens and wash leaves gently and thoroughly. Drain well and chop coarsely. Put greens in a salad bowl. Mix honey, garlic, red pepper flakes, and salt to taste in a small cup and add hot water. Stir until honey is dissolved, add yogurt, and pour over salad. Mix gently. Heat oil in a small pan or skillet; add fenugreek seeds and sauté until they soften, about 2 or 3 minutes. Pour over salad.

SERVES 4.

GREEN SALADS

Flexibility is the key to winter green salads. If you go shopping with your heart set on a Caesar, you might come home with a brownish head of romaine when you could have had a perfectly nice spinach salad for half the price. Likewise, gardeners need to head outdoors with an open mind. Unless you garden on a large scale or live alone, you are unlikely to have enough of any one green in December or January. When it comes to combinations, anything you like goes. Like the gourmet salad mixtures sold at some farmers markets and groceries, your salads will vary with the weather and your fancy.

I prefer rather simple salads, and I try for contrasting textures and complementary flavors. Arugula and corn salad make a nice mix of spicy and bland, and some chopped leeks or green onions give a little crunch. Arugula and mustard greens together would be overkill, unless you really like it hot and don't mind a coarse texture. Sorrel and spinach are an easy, pretty combination. The leaves are similar in shape and size, but the sorrel is a lighter green. I think most winter salads should be dressed with a fairly plain vinaigrette; more complicated dressings can clash with the many-flavored greens. But sorrel and spinach, alone or together, are good candidates for your favorite wilted salad.

Keep in mind that almost everything harvested in midwinter will taste stronger than the same plant in spring and summer. Also, even the toughest greens suffer some structural damage in freezing weather. They won't be as crisp as they were in October. Harvest and clean them very gently to avoid bruising.

WILTED GREENS SALAD

I'm not usually crazy about wilted salads, but I like this one a lot. The bacon drippings smooth out the strong tastes of the greens.

1 pound (about 6 cups) mixed greens—sorrel, spinach, mild mustards, dandelion, and so on—in which sorrel should predominate

3 strips bacon, diced

2 tablespoons lemon juice

2 tablespoons olive oil

1 tablespoon minced shallot or onion

pinch of dry mustard

hot pepper sauce

Wash greens, dry gently, and tear into bite-sized pieces. Be especially careful with the sorrel, which bruises easily. Sauté bacon until crisp. Remove it to drain on paper towels. Pour off bacon drippings; measure out 2 tablespoons and return to pan. Mix lemon juice, olive oil, shallot or onion, dry mustard, and a shake of hot pepper sauce in a small bowl. Reheat bacon drippings, add lemon juice and oil mixture, and heat through. Pour over greens just before serving.

SERVES 4.

HISTORIC SALAD

This updated 17th-century recipe is from Court and Country Cook, *an English translation of an early French cookbook. It is not for the faint of palate, but it's good. You could reduce or omit the anchovies and still have plenty of flavor.*

8 hard-boiled eggs

1 head Boston lettuce or other Bibb-type lettuce

1 fennel bulb, sliced

4 medium beets, baked or boiled, peeled, and chopped fine

8 anchovy fillets (optional)

2 teaspoons chopped parsley

1 teaspoon chopped fresh chervil (optional)

1 teaspoon chopped fresh tarragon or 1/2 teaspoon dried

1 teaspoon chopped chives

1 teaspoon chopped capers

1/4 cup olive oil

3 tablespoons red wine vinegar

Peel and quarter eggs. Line a salad bowl with lettuce leaves. Arrange eggs on lettuce, add fennel slices, sprinkle with chopped beets, and crisscross anchovies (if used) over the top. Put herbs and capers in a jar with a lid, add olive oil and vinegar, close tightly, and shake until blended. Pour over salad just before serving.

SERVES 8.

RAITAS

Raitas are yogurt-based accompaniments to Indian meals. They are simple to make and pretty, and they add immeasurably to a curry or pilaf. Most follow the same basic pattern, so it's easy to invent your own using carrots, cabbage, bananas, or whatever else sounds tasty. Raitas don't keep well; cut the recipes in half if leftovers are a problem.

Watercress Raita

1 cup watercress leaves, chopped

2 cups plain yogurt

1 clove garlic, chopped

pinch of cayenne

Combine watercress, yogurt, and garlic in a blender, or reduce watercress and garlic to a paste with a mortar and pestle and then stir in yogurt. (The raita will be thinner if you use a blender.) Sprinkle with cayenne and refrigerate until time to serve.

MAKES 2 CUPS.

Radish Raita

1 cup grated radish (red or daikon)

2 teaspoons salt

2 cups plain yogurt

1/8 teaspoon ground cumin

pinch of cayenne

Put grated radish in a bowl. Add salt and knead to squeeze out excess water. In another bowl, beat yogurt with a fork until smooth. Add radish and cumin and mix well. Sprinkle with cayenne and refrigerate until time to serve.

MAKES 2 CUPS.

SALAT

This contemporary-sounding salad is from the oldest known cookbook in English, The Forme of Cury ("cookery"), compiled around 1390. I think it has plenty of onion flavor, so I omit the 4 minced shallots called for in the original. Feel free to put them back. Borage is a fuzzy-leaved, blue-flowered herb that tastes like cucumber peels. I don't like it, but lots of people do.

1 bunch watercress (leaves only)

1 bulb fennel, sliced thin

1 clove garlic, minced

6 to 8 green onions, minced

2 leeks (white part only), sliced thin

1 teaspoon chopped fresh sage or ½ teaspoon dried

½ teaspoon dried borage (optional)

leaves from 1 sprig fresh rosemary, chopped

2 tablespoons minced parsley

3 tablespoons olive oil

2 tablespoons white wine vinegar

salt and pepper

Combine all vegetables and herbs in a salad bowl. Mix together oil, vinegar, salt, and pepper. Pour over salad, toss, and serve.

SERVES 4.

RUTACHOKE SALAD

Crisp sweet rutabaga and peppery radish perk up this attractive salad. Grate the Jerusalem artichoke last so that it doesn't discolor.

½ cup grated rutabaga

½ cup grated Jerusalem artichoke

2 green onions or small leeks, chopped

2 radishes, sliced thin

3 cups shredded romaine

Dressing

3 tablespoons olive oil

1 tablespoon wine vinegar

salt and pepper

¼ teaspoon dry mustard

¼ teaspoon dried basil

Combine vegetables in salad bowl and chill well. Combine dressing ingredients in a jar, shake, and chill. Dress and toss just before serving.

SERVES 4.

Spinach Salad with Pine Nut Dressing

Salads make the most of winter spinach, which generally doesn't grow fast enough to provide large quantities for cooking. The taste is a revelation, incomparably sweeter and richer than that of summer varieties. Sunflower seeds won't give the same effect as pine nuts, but they also make a good salad.

6 cups of spinach leaves, washed and carefully dried

$1/4$ cup pine nuts, chopped fine

$1/4$ cup olive oil

3 tablespoons tarragon vinegar

$1/4$ teaspoon grated lemon peel (optional)

$1/2$ teaspoon salt

Put spinach in a bowl. Combine remaining ingredients and pour over spinach. Toss gently.

SERVES 6.

Sprout Salad

You need sprouts with some body here; alfalfa sprouts are too tender. I favor the mixed sprout packages you can buy in many supermarkets. Otherwise, use sunflower or mung bean sprouts. Powdered ginger won't work in this recipe. If you use fresh ginger only occasionally, you can wrap the root tightly in plastic and freeze it. Remove from freezer (do not thaw), grate what you need, and return the rest to the cold. Frozen ginger will keep its flavor for about a month.

2 cups sprouts, rinsed

1 medium carrot, grated

1 small turnip, peeled and grated

2 minced shallots or 2 tablespoons minced onion

1 cup sliced mushrooms (optional)

2 tablespoons soy sauce

2 teaspoons grated ginger

3 tablespoons oil

2 tablespoons rice wine vinegar

1 tablespoon toasted sesame seeds

toasted sesame oil

Mix together sprouts, carrot, turnip, shallots or onion, and mushrooms (if used). Combine soy sauce, ginger, oil, and rice wine vinegar and pour over salad. Sprinkle with sesame seeds and a few shakes of sesame oil.

SERVES 4.

THAI BEEF AND RADISH SALAD

This is a wonderful introduction to the flavors of Thai cooking at home because it requires only one out-of-the-ordinary ingredient, fermented fish sauce. Also sold under the names nuoc mam *(Vietnamese) and* nam pla *(Thai), fish sauce has a raunchy smell and a surprisingly delicate taste. You can now find it in many regular supermarkets as well as any Asian food store. It's inexpensive and it keeps forever. The Thai sauce called for in this recipe is milder than Vietnamese* nuoc mam. *Greens can be varied to suit your larder, but the salad won't taste right without some fresh cilantro.*

Salad

1 bunch watercress leaves (about ½ cup packed), stemmed

½ cup fresh mint leaves

¼ cup fresh cilantro leaves

4 to 6 leaves Bibb or other leaf lettuce

½ pound julienned stir-fried beef or ½ pound julienned cold roast beef

1 small bunch red radishes, halved and sliced

1 small red onion, sliced thin

Mix greens together and put them on a serving dish. Arrange beef, radishes, and onions on top.

Dressing

3 tablespoons mild vegetable oil

2 tablespoons fresh lemon or lime juice

1 tablespoon Thai fish sauce or 2 teaspoons Vietnamese fish sauce

½ teaspoon sugar

½ teaspoon black pepper

¼ teaspoon dried hot pepper flakes

Put all ingredients in a jar. Cover and shake until combined. Pour over salad just before serving and toss lightly. Dressing will keep a few days in the refrigerator.

SERVES 4.

TURNIP SALAD

The Japanese are great connoisseurs of turnips, growing many varieties unfamiliar in North America. Small, crisp roots are what you want for salads such as these. The baseball-sized specimens at the supermarket are too hot and too corky to use raw. This salad is also good made with kohlrabi. Use a good-quality soy sauce.

1 pound small turnips

2 tablespoons sesame oil

1 teaspoon sugar

1/4 teaspoon ground ginger

2 tablespoons soy sauce

2 tablespoons cider vinegar

Peel turnips if necessary and cut into fine slivers. Mix with remaining ingredients and marinate for several hours.

SERVES 6.

MAIN DISHES

HOT PINK CANNELLONI

In Italy, vendors sell baked beets, ready to slice for salad with sweet onion, oil, and lemon or to use as a ravioli filling. I never seem to have time to make ravioli, so I use the same beet mixture for cannelloni. The baked beets can also be served as is. Lacking a handy Italian market, the beet baker's best friend is a microwave oven: 4 medium beets in ¼ cup of water take 15 minutes or a little more at high heat. The cooked beets can be frozen for future use. For a conventional oven, preheat to 350°F. Wrap each scrubbed but unpeeled beet in foil and bake until tender. Time will vary with the size of the beet, but count on at least 1½ hours, probably more. Do not undercook or the purée will be lumpy.

12 cannelloni

1 baked beet, about 10 ounces

1 egg

5 tablespoons butter, divided

½ pound ricotta

salt and pepper

½ cup dry bread crumbs

2 tablespoons flour

1 cup milk or half-and-half

salt and white pepper

freshly grated nutmeg

⅓ cup grated Parmesan cheese

Preheat oven to 350°. Cook cannelloni in boiling salted water until almost tender. Drain and place on a lightly oiled plate, separating tubes so they don't stick together. Peel and slice the cooked beet. Purée until smooth. Melt 3 tablespoons of the butter in a saucepan. Add beet purée and cook gently for about 10 minutes. Transfer to bowl and blend in ricotta, egg, and bread crumbs. Add salt and pepper to taste.

Melt remaining 2 tablespoons of butter in a small saucepan. Stir in flour and add milk or half-and-half. Bring just to boiling, reduce heat, and simmer gently until mixture is reduced to a sauce. Stir in salt, white pepper, and nutmeg to taste. While sauce is cooking, stuff cannelloni with beet mixture and place in lightly oiled baking dish, one layer deep. Pour sauce over and sprinkle with Parmesan cheese. Bake 30 minutes.

SERVES 4.

TURKISH CAULIFLOWER AND LENTIL STEW

 Rich flavor in a meatless entrée.

1½ pounds cauliflower, broken into florets

4 tablespoons olive oil

1 cup finely chopped onion

1 carrot, chopped fine

2 garlic cloves, chopped fine

2 tablespoons finely chopped fresh parsley

1 cup chopped Jerusalem artichoke (optional)

1 cup green or brown lentils

salt and pepper

¼ teaspoon cayenne

½ teaspoon ground allspice

½ cup undrained canned Italian plum tomatoes, chopped

1 tablespoon dried dill weed

Steam cauliflower until barely tender, about 7 minutes. Drain and set aside. Heat oil in a saucepan. Add onion, carrot, garlic, parsley, and Jerusalem artichoke (if used), and sauté over medium heat for 5 minutes. Add lentils, salt, pepper, cayenne, allspice, and vegetable broth or water and wine and simmer, covered, stirring occasionally, until lentils are just tender, about 30 minutes.

Place tomatoes in large saucepan; add cauliflower, lentils, and cooking liquid and simmer, covered, over very low heat for 30 minutes. Add water or broth during cooking as necessary, but do not stir the vegetables. Serve hot, sprinkled with dill.

SERVES 4 TO 6.

KALE MANICOTTI

Kale combines nicely with a mild cheese like ricotta. (It also is good simply steamed and served with béchamel). This simple manicotti filling, a specialty at the Innisfree restaurant in Glacier, Washington, also could be made with raab.

2 large bunches kale, ribs removed

1 pound ricotta cheese

1 cup grated Parmesan cheese, divided

1 egg, lightly beaten

1 teaspoon minced garlic

2 teaspoons chopped parsley

½ teaspoon paprika

1 teaspoon fresh basil or ½ teaspoon dried

nutmeg, salt, and white pepper to taste

½ pound fresh sheet pasta

1 cup tomato sauce

Preheat oven to 350°F. Steam kale briefly, no more than 2 minutes. Remove from steamer, squeeze out excess moisture, and chop coarsely. Mix together in a large bowl ricotta, ½ cup of the Parmesan cheese, egg, garlic, parsley, paprika, basil, nutmeg, salt, and white pepper. Add kale and mix well.

Cut sheet pasta into 4-inch squares. In a large pot of boiling water cook pasta al dente, 3 or 4 minutes. Drain and rinse in cold water until cool enough to handle. Lay a pasta square on a kitchen towel. Pat dry. Using about 2 tablespoons of cheese mixture, lay filling diagonally across square. Bring opposite corners of square up across filling, pressing edges together to seal.

Put a thin layer of tomato sauce in a 9-by-13-inch baking pan. Carefully lay the manicotti in the the pan and drizzle with more tomato sauce. Bake, covered, for about 25 minutes. Sprinkle with the remaining ½ cup of Parmesan cheese and serve.

SERVES 4.

HAZELNUT, CHARD, AND GOAT CHEESE FILO PIE

The kitchen staff at Sooke Harbour House on Vancouver Island has modified a recipe by Stewart Barnes to make this savory variation on spanakopita. They use red-stemmed ruby chard. Regular green chard or the traditional spinach may be substituted.

¼ package filo pastry

3 medium leeks, white part only, sliced thin

3 tablespoons unsalted butter

2 cloves garlic, chopped fine

1 teaspoon finely chopped English thyme or ½ teaspoon dried

2 teaspoons finely chopped marjoram or ¾ teaspoon dried

¼ cup dry white wine

3 large bunches Swiss chard or spinach, leaves only, washed and shredded

½ pound creamy goat's-milk cheese

2 eggs, beaten

¾ cup melted clarified butter

1 cup roasted crushed hazelnuts

1 tablespoon chopped chives

1 tablespoon chopped fennel leaves

1 tablespoon chopped rosemary

Preheat oven to 350°F. If using frozen filo, remove pastry from freezer and let thaw while making filling. When thawed, unfold dough and cut in half crosswise. Melt the 3 tablespoons of butter and sauté leeks for 2 or 3 minutes. Add garlic, thyme, marjoram, and white wine. Cook, covered, until leeks are soft. Add chard or spinach and cook, uncovered, until greens are wilted and liquid has reduced by half. Pour mixture into a bowl. Add goat cheese and eggs and mix thoroughly.

Mix together chopped chives, fennel, and rosemary. Brush a 9-by-13-inch pan with some of the melted clarified butter and place a sheet of filo on the bottom. Brush with butter and sprinkle with hazelnuts and mixed herbs. Continue layering with butter, herbs, and hazelnuts for 10 sheets. Spoon spinach and cheese mixture evenly across pan. Continue with layers of filo, butter, and herbs 10 more times. Brush final layer with butter. Sprinkle herbs on top. Bake 40 to 45 minutes, until well browned.

SERVES 6.

RUSSIAN VEGETABLE PIE

Great for lunch, this dish makes plain ingredients taste special. Variations are just about infinite. You need some cream cheese, some mushrooms, and something in the cabbage family, but other additions (cooked carrots, celeriac, almonds or hazelnuts, steamed salsify) and substitutions are welcome.

Pastry

1¼ cups flour

1 teaspoon salt

2 tablespoons butter

4 ounces cream cheese

Sift together flour and salt. Cut in butter until mixture is the size of peas. Work in cream cheese and form pastry into two balls, one twice as big as the other. Chill until vegetables are ready. Then roll out the bigger ball and line a 9- or 10-inch pie pan. Roll out the remaining ball for the top crust.

Filling

4 tablespoons oil, divided

3 cups shredded green or red cabbage (1 small cabbage)

1 medium onion, chopped

2 cups sliced mushrooms

salt and pepper

½ teaspoon dried dill weed

¼ teaspoon fresh thyme or ⅛ teaspoon dried

4 ounces softened cream cheese

Preheat oven to 400°F. Heat 2 tablespoons of the oil in a large skillet or saucepan. Add cabbage and onion and sauté for 10 minutes. Heat remaining 2 tablespoons oil in another skillet or pan. Add mushrooms, salt, pepper, dill, and thyme and sauté for 5 minutes.

Spread cream cheese in bottom of pie shell. Spread cabbage and onion mixture evenly over cream cheese and follow with mushrooms. Cover with top crust. Make some decorative cuts in the top crust. Bake 15 minutes at 400°, reduce heat to 350°, and bake another 20 to 25 minutes. Cool a few minutes before serving.

SERVES 6.

DEEP-DISH HAZELNUT VEGETABLE PIE

At the end of Holmquist Road a few miles from my house is a hazelnut orchard. You can really taste the difference in freshness when you buy straight from the farm. Natalie and Gerald Holmquist, the proprietors, have devised a number of excellent recipes for their cash crop.

¾ cup cauliflower, in small florets

¾ cup broccoli, in small florets

2 cups chopped fresh or frozen spinach

1 small onion, chopped

1 or 2 cloves garlic, chopped

¾ cup grated Cheddar cheese

1 cup coarsely chopped hazelnuts

1½ cups milk

1 cup biscuit mix

3 eggs

salt and pepper

Preheat oven to 400°F. Steam cauliflower and broccoli until almost tender. Drain and mix with spinach, onion, garlic, and Cheddar cheese. Spoon mixture into well-greased 10-inch pie pan or baking dish. Top with hazelnuts. Beat together milk, biscuit mix, eggs, salt, and pepper. Pour over hazelnuts and vegetables and bake 35 to 40 minutes.

SERVES 6.

PIZZAS

The nouvelle pizza craze proved that just about anything that can be balanced on a crust and baked can be sold, at least once. Now that the air has cleared, we can concentrate on what actually tastes good thereon. My local pizza parlor has abandoned its forays into trendy territory—Exotic-Style ("two colors of cheese") and Macho Sauce (salsa) —but I still like to experiment at home. Many regional pizza favorites employ winter produce, and other combinations await your inspiration.

A major impediment to homemade pizza for busy people has been that the time required to make the crust cancels out the quick assembly and cooking. Fortunately, you can now buy partially baked crusts at the supermarket. Do-it-yourselfers can make their own dough in advance. It will keep in the refrigerator for a day and in the freezer for a month. Also, if you make your own dough you can indulge your show-biz fantasies by tossing and twirling it inches from the kitchen ceiling.

Basic pizza dough

A flavorful olive oil gives this crust extra presence. This is my favorite homemade crust.

1 cup warm water

2 teaspoons dry yeast

1 teaspoon salt

4 tablespoons olive oil

2³/₄ cups bread flour

Put warm water in large bowl. Sprinkle yeast over the surface, let it sit for 3 or 4 minutes, and then mix. Add salt and oil and mix again. Stir in flour and begin kneading in the bowl. When the sticky dough begins to pull away from the sides of the bowl, turn onto a floured surface and knead until silky, another 10 or 12 minutes. Add as little flour as possible to get a manageable dough.

Return dough to a clean, lightly floured bowl. Cover with a kitchen towel and let rise in a warm, draft-free place until doubled in size, at least 2 hours. Punch down dough. (At this point you can refrigerate the dough for up to a day or freeze it in an airtight container for up to a month. Remove from refrigerator half an hour before using and from freezer 2 hours before using.) Separate dough into balls if you are making more than one pizza. Roll into desired shape. Dough should be no more than ¼ inch thick. Place dough on ungreased pan, top, and bake.

MAKES 1 LARGE OR 8 INDIVIDUAL PIZZAS.

Campania Pizza

This highly flavored treat is traditional to the Christmas season in the Italian region of Campania.

20 cured Italian olives, pitted and coarsely chopped

4 tablespoons pine nuts

4 tablespoons raisins, coarsely chopped

2 tablespoons capers, coarsely chopped

1 medium head chicory or escarole

olive oil

8 anchovy fillets, chopped into small pieces

Preheat oven to 500°F. Put chopped olives in a medium bowl. Brown pine nuts carefully in a bare skillet over medium-low heat. Don't let them burn. Add to olives, along with raisins and capers, and stir.

Chop chicory or escarole roughly and boil in a small amount of water until tender, about 5 minutes. Drain chicory well (the cooking water is good in soup) and spread to cool. Once chicory is cool, wrap in a towel and squeeze out as much water as you can.

Cook anchovies briefly in about 2 tablespoons olive oil over medium heat. Add chicory and mix well. Use a bit more oil if necessary. Cook gently about 5 minutes. Let cool.

Roll out pizza dough to fit your pan. Drizzle on a little olive oil and then spread the anchovy and chicory mixture. Sprinkle on some salt and pepper and drizzle some more olive oil. Bake at bottom of oven for about 7 minutes. Serve hot.

SERVES 6 TO 8.

Leek and Olive Pizza

Pungent olives and sweet cooked leeks combine for a simple topping. The dried tomatoes are a nice touch. I dry some of my own each summer in a simple food drier. (See Other Ingredients section of Vegetable List.)

pizza dough

3 tablespoons olive oil

6 medium leeks, chopped, with an inch of green

2 tablespoons chopped dried tomatoes (optional)

20 Italian olives, pitted and chopped

3 tablespoons Parmesan cheese

Preheat oven to 500°F. Heat olive oil in a medium skillet. Add leeks and sauté gently for about 15 minutes. The leeks are taking the place of tomato sauce, so let them get really soft. Add dried tomatoes, if used, in the last 5 minutes of cooking. Spread mixture onto pizza dough. Sprinkle with chopped olives and Parmesan cheese and bake about 7 minutes on the bottom shelf.

SERVES 4 TO 6.

CABBAGE WITH NOODLES AND POPPY SEEDS

This Russian dish tastes even better the next day.

6 tablespoons butter, divided

1 small green cabbage, coarsely chopped

1 onion, coarsely chopped

2 small, tart apples, peeled, cored, and coarsely chopped

salt and pepper

½ pound dry fettuccine

2 tablespoons poppy seeds

Melt 4 tablespoons of the butter in a large skillet. Add cabbage, onion, and apples, stirring well. Add salt and pepper to taste, cover skillet, and simmer about 20 minutes or until soft. Add water if necessary to keep mixture from burning.

Cook fettuccine al dente. Drain. Stir in remaining 2 tablespoons butter and coat noodles well. Add cabbage mixture to noodles and mix carefully. Stir in poppy seeds and serve.

SERVES 6.

LINGUINE WITH BROCCOLI, CAULIFLOWER, AND MUSHROOMS

Simple and quick, this dish counts on really fresh vegetables for its flavor. If you grow overwintered broccoli and cauliflower, it can be one of the first treats of spring.

1 cup ricotta

⅓ cup grated Romano cheese

1 teaspoon salt

1 medium head broccoli, peeled and trimmed

1 medium head cauliflower, separated into florets

½ cup olive oil

6 cloves garlic, minced

1 pound mushrooms, sliced thin

2 teaspoons salt

½ teaspoon red pepper flakes

1 pound linguine

Combine ricotta and Romano in a small bowl and set aside. Add broccoli and cauliflower to boiling salted water in a large pot. Cook uncovered until vegetables are almost tender, about 5 to 7 minutes. Remove vegetables with slotted spoon. Keep liquid for cooking linguine.

Heat olive oil and garlic in a large, heavy skillet. When garlic is lightly browned, stir in mushrooms, salt, and red pepper flakes and sauté about 5 minutes. Stir in broccoli and cauliflower and continue cooking 10 minutes. Add some of the cooking water if mixture seems too dry.

Bring cooking water to a rapid boil, adding more water if needed. Add linguine and cook, uncovered, about 10 to 12 minutes. Drain. Reheat vegetables. Stir in linguine, divide among shallow bowls, and top with cheese mixture and some more grated Romano.

SERVES 4 AS A MAIN DISH
OR 6 AS A FIRST COURSE.

HARICOT MÉLANGE

Simple flavors simmer into a satisfying harmony. The type of beans matters. I tried this with pintos once, and it just wasn't the same.

6 cups water

½ pound dry white beans or small limas

2½ pounds Swiss chard (3 or 4 bunches), stems removed

¼ cup olive oil

1 small onion, coarsely chopped

6 to 8 canned tomatoes, drained and coarsely chopped

3 medium cloves garlic, chopped

¼ teaspoon dried basil

½ teaspoon fresh thyme or ¼ teaspoon dried

salt and pepper

Bring water to boil in a saucepan, add beans, and boil 2 minutes. Remove from heat and let stand 1 hour. Return to boil, reduce heat, and simmer until beans are tender, about 1½ hours. Drain.

Wash chard, shake off extra water, and cook in a large saucepan over high heat until wilted, 3 to 4 minutes. Stir frequently so it doesn't scorch. Drain well, squeeze dry, and chop coarsely.

Heat olive oil in heavy skillet over medium heat. Add onion and sauté until softened. Stir in beans, chard, tomatoes, garlic, basil, and thyme. Add salt and pepper to taste. Reduce heat and simmer 15 minutes to blend flavors, stirring frequently. Adjust seasoning and serve.

SERVES 6.

BAKED JERUSALEM ARTICHOKES WITH MUSHROOMS

This has a sweet, earthy taste, which will vary with the type of mushrooms. If you gather your own, you can use Northwest Boletus edulis, fresh or dried; they're the same species as the pricey porcini.

up to ¹/₂ cup dried porcini mushrooms (optional)

2 cups water, or light stock if no dried mushrooms are used

2 pounds Jerusalem artichokes, scrubbed

3 strips bacon or 2 tablespoons oil

1 onion, chopped

sliced mushrooms to total 2 cups with porcini

¹/₄ teaspoon nutmeg

¹/₄ teaspoon ginger

salt and pepper

¹/₂ cup grated Swiss cheese

1 tablespoon butter

Preheat oven to 450°F. Soak dried mushrooms (if used) in water for an hour; remove mushrooms and slice. Pour mushroom water or stock into a saucepan, heat to boiling, and add artichokes. Simmer until artichokes are tender but not mushy. Drain artichokes, peel, and chop coarsely.

Fry bacon or heat oil in a medium skillet. Remove bacon (if used) and pour off excess drippings. Add chopped onion and sauté until it begins to soften. Add soaked and fresh mushrooms and sauté another 2 or 3 minutes. Combine artichokes, mushrooms, onions, bacon (if used), nutmeg, ginger, salt, and pepper in a medium bowl.

Grease a casserole with bacon grease or a little butter. Spread on a layer of artichokes and onion and sprinkle with grated Swiss cheese. Make additional layers, ending with cheese. Dot with butter and bake for about 20 minutes.

SERVES 4.

BROCCOLI DAL CURRY

If you can get pink Indian lentils, they make a nice display with the bright green broccoli. Brown lentils don't look as exciting, but the range of textures still gives this meal extra interest.

1 cup lentils

4 tablespoons ghee (see page 218) or light oil

2 medium onions, chopped fine

1 teaspoon chili powder

2 teaspoons black pepper

1½ teaspoons ground cumin

1½ teaspoons ground coriander seeds

2 teaspoons turmeric

juice of half a lemon

2 medium heads broccoli

2 cups water

½ cup unsweetened dried coconut

1 tablespoon flour

1 teaspoon salt

1 cup cashews or roasted peanuts

Wash lentils well and drain. Heat ghee or oil in a large saucepan and sauté onions until they begin to soften. Add chili powder, black pepper, cumin, coriander, and turmeric. Stir and cook briefly. Add lentils, stir well, and add lemon juice, water, and coconut. Bring to a boil, reduce heat, and simmer about 25 to 30 minutes or until lentils are soft.

Meanwhile, cut broccoli into individual florets. (Save stems for another use.) Steam 5 or 10 minutes, until almost tender. Plunge broccoli in cold water, drain, and set aside.

Remove ⅓ cup of liquid from the lentil mixture, add to flour to form a smooth paste, and return it to the pan. Add steamed broccoli, salt, and nuts. Simmer another 5 to 10 minutes, until the lentils make a thick sauce. Serve with steamed basmati rice.

SERVES 4.

SPICY SQUASH STEW WITH CORNMEAL DUMPLINGS

A variation on a recipe from Anna Thomas's Vegetarian Epicure, Book Two, *this combines familiar Mexican flavors in a fresh and delicious way. All it needs is a salad and maybe a beer.*

1 cup sliced onion

4 tablespoons olive oil

6 cloves garlic, peeled and minced

3/4 teaspoon ground cumin

3/4 teaspoon cinnamon

3/4 cup diced, seeded hot green chiles (adjust amount and firepower to your taste)

7 cups (two 28-ounce cans) canned tomatoes

1 pound winter squash, peeled and cut into 1/2-inch cubes

1 1/2 teaspoons salt

1 1/2 cups water

1/2 pound mushrooms, quartered

3 tablespoons chopped cilantro

Sauté onion in olive oil in a large, wide pot until transparent. Add garlic, cumin, cinnamon, and chiles. Sauté a few minutes more, stirring constantly. Chop tomatoes coarsely and add them with their liquid, squash, salt, and water. Lower heat, cover pot, and simmer gently for about 1 hour. Add mushrooms and cilantro and simmer another 5 minutes. Drop dumpling batter (see recipe below) on stew by teaspoonfuls, cover pot tightly, and simmer over very low heat for 20 minutes.

Dumplings

1 cup yellow cornmeal

1/3 cup white flour

1 teaspoon baking powder

3/4 teaspoon salt

1 teaspoon sugar

1 egg

1/2 cup half-and-half or milk

1 1/2 tablespoons melted butter

Sift together cornmeal, flour, baking powder, salt, and sugar. Beat together egg and half-and-half or milk and stir into dry mixture. Add melted butter and stir until batter is smooth. Add to stew right away, and serve as soon as dumplings are done.

MAKES 2 DOZEN DUMPLINGS.
SERVES 6 TO 8.

NETTLE OMELET

On our farm, chickens come out of their winter egg-laying slump about the time the new nettle crop is 3 or 4 inches tall. A nettle omelet is one of our spring rituals. Wear rubber gloves when harvesting and preparing nettles, and use the leaves only. I stop harvesting when they are about 8 inches tall; mature plants are too stringy.

4 cups nettle leaves, loosely packed

½ cup ricotta

5 tablespoons butter, divided

2 shallots, minced, or 2 tablespoons minced onion

5 eggs, beaten

salt and pepper

pinch of fresh tarragon

Steam nettle leaves until limp. Remove from heat, press out moisture, and chop. Mix with ricotta and set aside. Melt 1 tablespoon butter in a small saucepan, add shallots or onion, cook gently until they start to turn color, and stir them into nettle mixture. Add salt and pepper to beaten eggs. Melt remaining butter in an omelet pan or your closest approximation. Add eggs and cook over low heat, loosening edges as they solidify and letting uncooked egg run under. Spoon ricotta-nettle mixture onto one half of the omelet, leaving a 2-inch margin bare. Slide a spatula gently under the other half and fold omelet over filling. Cook very gently, about 2 minutes on each side, sprinkle with tarragon, and serve hot.

SERVES 2 OR 3.

SUNDAY BRUNCH FRITTATA

This dish is the perfect antidote to too much wholesome oatmeal. The smaller the pan, the thicker and puffier the result and the longer the cooking time. Purists might want to turn the almost-finished frittata onto a plate and then slide it back upside-down into the pan for the last minute of cooking. I find it easier to finish it under the broiler, which also means that I can show off a decorative pattern of vegetables on top.

⅓ cup light oil

2 leeks, with some green, trimmed and sliced into thin rounds

3 medium Jerusalem artichokes, scrubbed and sliced thin

½ cup parsley, chopped

2 tablespoons fresh cilantro

1 teaspoon dried basil

6 eggs

⅓ cup milk

⅓ cup sour cream

salt and pepper

1 cup grated Muenster or Monterey jack cheese

Heat oil in a large skillet and sauté leeks and Jerusalem artichokes over medium-low heat until soft, 5 to 7 minutes. Add parsley, cilantro, and basil and sauté 2 more minutes. Remove mixture from pan and set aside.

Beat eggs in medium bowl. Beat in milk, sour cream, salt, and pepper. Return skillet to burner and heat to medium. Add egg mixture and reduce heat to low. Spread vegetable mixture evenly over eggs and cover with cheese.

Cook gently until eggs have set on bottom and top is just slightly soupy. Place skillet under broiler with door ajar and cook until top is golden and puffy. Serve at once.

SERVES 3 OR 4.

INDIAN SPINACH WITH POTATOES

This is quick and good. If you boil the potatoes beforehand, you can have dinner on the table in about 10 minutes. You can adjust the spiciness according to the type of chili powder you use, and by the addition of red pepper flakes. Serve with Carrot Curry (page 172) and a Raita (page 100) for a beautiful and nutritious vegetarian meal. The ¼ cup of oil seems like a lot, but it is needed to coat the potatoes.

2 pounds boiled peeled potatoes

1 pound spinach

¼ cup peanut or other light oil

1 cup chopped onion

1 or 2 cloves garlic, minced

1-inch piece fresh ginger, peeled and sliced thin

1 teaspoon mustard seed

1 teaspoon ground cumin

red pepper flakes (optional)

1 teaspoon turmeric

½ teaspoon chili powder

1 teaspoon salt, or to taste

Cut potatoes into cubes. You should have about 4 cups. Chop spinach coarsely. Heat oil in a large saucepan, add onion, garlic, and fresh ginger, and sauté briefly. Combine mustard seed, cumin, red pepper flakes (if used), turmeric, and chili powder. Add to saucepan, stir well, and cook mixture over gentle heat until onion is soft.

Add potatoes and stir gently to coat them with spices. Add spinach in handfuls. Add salt, stir again carefully but thoroughly, cover, and cook 3 minutes or so, until spinach is cooked down a bit. Serve at once.

SERVES 4 TO 6.

CHARD TART

This meatless version of Judie Geise's recipe in The Northwest Kitchen *tastes richer than it is, and the green-flecked, golden pie is attractive. It is a good use for somewhat weatherbeaten winter chard.*

1 pound Swiss chard

lemon juice

2 tablespoons olive oil

1 medium onion, chopped fine

2 cloves garlic, chopped fine

salt and pepper

freshly grated nutmeg

1½ cups ricotta

½ cup plus 1 tablespoon Parmesan cheese, divided

½ cup milk

3 eggs, beaten

partially baked pastry shell

Preheat oven to 350°F. Remove chard stems, wash leaves, and blanch 2 to 3 minutes in salted water with a squeeze of lemon. Leaves should be tender but still bright green. Drain, rinse with cold water, squeeze dry, and chop into shreds.

Heat olive oil in a medium skillet. Add onion and sauté a few minutes. Do not let it brown. Add chard and garlic and cook over medium-high heat for 5 minutes or until moisture is absorbed. Be careful that it doesn't scorch. Sprinkle with salt, pepper, and nutmeg and remove from heat.

Stir ricotta in mixing bowl. Add milk, beaten eggs, and ½ cup of the Parmesan cheese and blend until smooth. Stir in chard mixture and adjust seasoning.

Pour into pastry shell, sprinkle with remaining Parmesan, and bake about 40 minutes. Cool slightly before serving.

SERVES 6.

STUFFED SAVOY

A savoy's thinner leaves make it easier to roll than regular cabbage, and its delicate flavor is well suited to this meatless stuffing. If you grow your own mint, you can extend its season by bringing in a bunch in the fall and letting it root in a jar of water on the windowsill.

1 medium savoy cabbage

⅓ cup olive oil

1 cup chopped Jerusalem artichoke

1 medium onion, chopped fine

3 cloves garlic, chopped

2 cups stewed tomatoes, drained and chopped

2 cups cooked brown rice

¼ cup chopped fresh mint or 1 tablespoon dried

1 teaspoon cinnamon

salt and pepper

¾ cup ricotta

Preheat oven to 350°F. Carefully separate 12 cabbage leaves, trimming the thickest part of the rib. Steam until pliable, about 5 minutes. Heat oil in large frying pan, add Jerusalem artichokes, onion, and garlic, and cook over low heat until artichokes are almost tender, 5 to 7 minutes. Add 1½ cups of the tomatoes, rice, and mint. Cover and simmer about 20 minutes until most of the liquid is gone. Add cinnamon for last 5 minutes of cooking. Season with salt and pepper to taste.

Put a cabbage leaf on a lightly oiled plate, mound about 3 tablespoons of stuffing near the base, and roll into a neat package. Place roll, seam side down, in oiled baking pan. Repeat.

Mix ricotta with the remaining ½ cup tomatoes and spread over top of rolls. Bake 30 minutes, uncovered.

SERVES 6 TO 8.

FEIJOADA

A real Brazilian feijoada is a major project. It requires dried beef, smoked tongue, hot sausage, salt pork, and a long siesta afterwards. The vegetarian version presented by Frances Moore Lappé in Diet for a Small Planet *is much simpler to make and probably closer to what is eaten outside the most affluent circles. I love it. You can use lard or bacon drippings instead of oil and cook the beans in beef stock if you want a more authentic flavor. This is a complete meal. Finish it off with some strong, sweet coffee and a flan if you want to maintain a Brazilian feel.*

Beans

1 large onion, chopped

2 cloves garlic, chopped

oil

1 cup dry black (turtle) beans

3 cups stock (or substitute white wine for half the stock)

1 bay leaf

salt and pepper

1 whole peeled orange

2 stalks celery or Swiss chard stems, chopped

1 canned tomato, drained and chopped

Sauté onion and garlic in a little oil in a deep, heavy pot. Add beans, cover with stock, and add bay leaf. Bring to a boil, simmer 2 minutes, turn off heat, and let stand, covered, for an hour. Add orange, celery or chard, tomato, salt, and pepper. Bring back to a boil and simmer, covered, for 2 to 3 hours, until beans are tender. Remove a ladleful of beans, mash them, and return to the pot. Cook gently, stirring often, until mixture begins to thicken.

Rice

1 onion, chopped

3 cloves garlic, minced

2 tablespoons vegetable oil

2 tablespoons butter or lard

2 canned tomatoes, drained, seeded, and chopped

2 cups cooked rice

Sauté onion and garlic in oil and butter until golden. Add tomatoes and cooked rice and warm over low heat.

Salsa

1 frozen tomato (see Other Ingredients section of Vegetable List), thawed and skinned

1 jalapeño or other green chile, seeded (more if you like it hot)

1 teaspoon salt

2 cloves garlic, crushed

juice of 1 lemon

1 small onion, chopped

1 tablespoon finely chopped cilantro or parsley

2 green onions or equivalent amount of chives, chopped

1/4 cup red wine vinegar

Put the tomato, chile, salt, and garlic in a blender and purée. Pour into serving bowl, add remaining ingredients, and stir. Just before serving, stir in a little liquid from the bean pot.

Greens

1 1/2 pounds sturdy greens, trimmed and coarsely chopped (collards are traditional)

1 clove garlic, minced

1 tablespoon olive oil

4 tablespoons toasted sesame seeds

1 orange, peeled and sliced

Steam greens until tender. (Time will vary according to what kind of greens you use.) Meanwhile, sauté garlic in olive oil. Add steamed greens and sauté, stirring, for no more than a minute. Put mixture in serving dish, sprinkle with sesame seeds, and arrange orange slices on top.

SERVES 4.

SORREL AND LEEK BAKE

The first spring sorrel comes up while overwintered leeks are still in their prime. This Swiss-Italian dish was no doubt a gardener's creation. If you are using wild sorrel rather than garden sorrel, decrease the amount by about 25 percent to compensate for its stronger taste.

4 eggs

1/2 teaspoon salt

1/4 teaspoon pepper

1 1/2 cups water

1 cup yellow cornmeal

1 pound French sorrel, coarsely chopped

1 pound leeks (about 4 medium), white part only, sliced thin

3/4 cup grated Swiss cheese

5 tablespoons olive oil, divided

2 tablespoons grated Parmesan cheese

Preheat oven to 375°F. Beat eggs in a small bowl until light. Add salt and pepper. In a medium bowl, add cold water gradually to cornmeal, stirring constantly until it is well mixed. Stir in eggs, and then stir in sorrel, leeks, and Swiss cheese.

Grease a large, shallow casserole or baking dish with 2 tablespoons of the oil. Pour in vegetable mixture, level top, and sprinkle with Parmesan cheese. Dribble remaining oil on top. Bake 50 to 60 minutes until set.

SERVES 3 AS A MAIN DISH OR 4 AS A SIDE DISH.

MEXICAN CHARD AND POTATOES

Chard is a common green in Mexico, where it tolerates both the heat of the lowlands and the chill of the mountains. This versatile dish can be served as is or adapted to whatever extras are around the kitchen. Cubes of queso fresco, *a mild cooking cheese somewhat like the Indian* panir, *can be added along with the chard. You can also add leftover pork or shredded beef. Rick Bayless, who got this recipe from a traditional Mexican cookbook, also suggests it as a taco filling. Epazote* (Chenopodium ambrosioides) *is a common cooking herb in southern Mexico and the Yucatán. A member of the same genus as Good King Henry and lamb's-quarters, it is available from some herb suppliers. The dried leaves sold in Mexican groceries unfortunately don't have much flavor.*

1 tablespoon cooking oil

1 small onion, sliced thin

1 fresh serrano chile or half a jalapeño chile, stemmed, seeded, and sliced thin

2 whole canned tomatoes

$^{1}/_{2}$ pound potatoes (preferably thin-skinned boiling types), peeled and cubed (about 2 cups)

$^{1}/_{2}$ cup chicken or beef stock or water

4 leaves epazote (optional)

$^{1}/_{2}$ teaspoon salt

2 cups Swiss chard leaves, sliced crosswise in 1-inch strips

Heat oil in a medium saucepan. Add onion and chile and cook, stirring frequently, until onion is lightly browned, 7 or 8 minutes. Chop tomatoes, add to pan, and cook 3 or 4 minutes longer to reduce the liquid a little.

Stir in potatoes, stock or water, epazote (if used), and salt. Cover and cook over medium-low heat until potatoes are tender, about 10 minutes. Check the amount of liquid and add more if necessary; there should be about ¼ cup.

Add chard, cover, and cook over medium heat until tender, about 3 minutes. Uncover and taste for salt. There should be enough sauce to coat the vegetables. Serve immediately.

SERVES 4.

Italian Spinach and Rice Pie

A simple risotto is baked with eggs in a crumb crust. The result slices well and is excellent for potlucks and tailgate picnics. If you have lots of top-quality fresh spinach, by all means use it.

3½ cups chicken broth

two 10-ounce packages frozen spinach or 3 pounds fresh

4 tablespoons olive oil

½ cup pancetta or blanched bacon, chopped

¼ cup chopped onion

1 large clove garlic, chopped

1 cup rice, preferably Arborio or other short-grained variety

2 tablespoons butter

⅓ cup dry bread crumbs

4 eggs

½ cup grated Parmesan cheese

1 teaspoon dried marjoram

½ teaspoon freshly grated nutmeg

salt and pepper

Simmer broth over low heat. If you are using frozen spinach, it's easier to chop when partially thawed. Continue thawing, pressing excess moisture into heated broth. If you are using fresh spinach, steam leaves until soft, about 2 minutes. Remove from heat, chop, and press excess moisture into broth. Heat olive oil in large skillet over medium heat and sauté pancetta or bacon, onion, and garlic for 5 to 10 minutes. Mix in rice and cook 2 to 3 minutes, stirring constantly.

Reduce heat, stir in spinach, and bring to slow simmer. Cook, covered, adding broth ½ cup at a time, stirring frequently and allowing rice to absorb broth before adding more. This will take about 20 to 25 minutes. Rice should be creamy. Remove cover and let cool to room temperature.

Preheat oven to 350°F. Butter a 9-inch quiche dish or pie plate and sprinkle with bread crumbs. Shake off excess crumbs and reserve for topping.

Combine eggs, Parmesan cheese, marjoram, nutmeg, salt, and pepper in a large mixing bowl and beat well. Stir in rice mixture. Taste and adjust seasoning. Spoon into quiche dish or pie plate, spreading evenly. Sprinkle top with remaining bread crumbs. Bake until firm but not dry, about 45 minutes to 1 hour. Cool before serving.

SERVES 5 AS A MAIN DISH OR 8 AS A SIDE DISH.

PORK CHOPS WITH MARINADE

This quick dinner, from Elizabeth David's Mediterranean Food, *can vary deliciously through the seasons, depending on the herbs and greens available.*

1 pork chop per diner

½ cup chopped herbs—fennel, parsley, chives, and so on

salt and pepper

garlic, chopped, 1 clove for every 2 chops

1 tablespoon olive oil per chop

1 tablespoon lemon juice per chop

Trim fat from pork chops. Place chops in shallow bowl or baking pan and cover with herbs and garlic. Sprinkle with salt and pepper. Drizzle on olive oil and lemon juice and leave chops to marinate at least an hour.

Broil chops or cook over an electric grill, basting with herbs and marinade. Serve with a green salad upon which, instead of dressing, you have poured the juices and herbs which have fallen from the meat into the broiling pan.

English Turnip Casserole

Contrary to popular belief, British cooks do not spend all their time boiling Brussels sprouts to death. Hearty casseroles and meat pies are a worthy part of English provincial cooking.

3 pounds young turnips (about a dozen)

1/4 cup butter, divided

1/4 pound smoked ham, cut into cubes

salt and pepper

1 1/4 cups half-and-half

1 1/2 cups fresh white bread crumbs

1 cup grated Cheddar cheese

Preheat oven to 400°F. Scrub turnips and steam over boiling water until almost tender, about 20 minutes. Remove from heat and set aside until cool enough to handle. Then peel and cut into 1/4-inch cubes.

Melt 2 tablespoons of the butter in a small skillet; add ham and brown 1 or 2 minutes. Use drippings to grease a shallow casserole or baking dish. Make alternate layers of turnips and ham, seasoning each layer with salt and pepper to taste. Pour in half-and-half. Mix bread crumbs and Cheddar cheese and sprinkle over top. Melt remaining 2 tablespoons butter and drizzle over crumb mixture. Bake about 15 minutes, until browned and bubbling, or broil, watching carefully so that it does not burn.

SERVES 4.

Kale, Bacon, and Potatoes

This combination is popular among the many Dutch immigrants in my community. Preparation time is about 30 seconds, there are no extra pots and pans to wash, and it tastes great. It's an excellent choice for tough old kale. Use thick-sliced bacon. Thin-skinned potatoes can be left unpeeled.

Line the bottom of a heavy skillet with bacon. Cover bacon with a layer of potatoes, which can be left whole if they are small, or quartered or sliced if they are larger. Wash kale, shake off excess water but do not dry, and chop. Cram in as much chopped kale as will fit on top of the potatoes. Cover and cook very slowly over low heat. Check after an hour. The bacon and potatoes should be crisp, and the kale should be soft in the middle of the pan and a little crisp around the edges.

ROMEO CONCA'S PORK CHOPS AND KALE

Romeo Conca, proprietor of Lost Mountain Winery on the Olympic Peninsula, is a wonderful cook. This delicious dinner is ridiculously easy, and it proves that kale has more going for it than hardiness and nutrition.

kale

1 pork chop per diner

dry mustard

black pepper

salt

olive oil

garlic, chopped, 1 clove for every 2 chops

Wash kale and remove any heavy stems. Pat pork chops dry. Dust one side lightly with dry mustard and grind on some pepper.

Coat the bottom of a heavy skillet with olive oil and heat to the smoking point. Salt the spiced side of the chops and cook, seasoned side down, until lightly browned. Salt top sides and turn.

Reduce heat to medium-low and cook until chops feel firm to the touch. Sprinkle in garlic and add as much kale as will fit in the pan. You can really cram it in. Drizzle in a little more olive oil and cover with tight-fitting lid. Lower heat to simmer and cook until kale is limp. Cooking time will vary with the maturity of the kale.

ITALIAN SAUSAGE WITH FENNEL, CARROT, AND CABBAGE

1 cup dry white wine

1½ to 2 pounds Italian link sausages

1 medium onion, minced

1 large carrot, julienned

4 cups coarsely chopped cabbage

2 large fennel bulbs, sliced thin

3 tablespoons minced fennel leaves, divided

1 garlic clove, minced

½ cup water

salt and pepper

Bring wine to boil in a large, heavy skillet. Prick each sausage in several places with fork and add to skillet. Reduce heat, cover, and simmer gently for 15 minutes. Remove cover and continue simmering until wine has evaporated. Then increase heat and brown sausage quickly. Remove sausages and keep warm.

Pour off all but 4 or 5 tablespoons fat from skillet. Turn heat to medium-high. Add onion and carrot and cook, stirring often, about 5 minutes. Stir in cabbage, sliced fennel, 2 tablespoons of the fennel leaves, garlic, and water. Cover and cook until vegetables are barely tender, about 3 to 5 minutes. Remove cover and boil off any liquid remaining in skillet. Remove from heat and adjust seasoning.

Make a bed of the vegetables on a serving platter. Arrange sausages on top, sprinkle with remaining fennel leaves, and serve.

SERVES 4 TO 6.

PARSNIPS AND SAUSAGE

This dish can be mild or zippy depending on the sausage seasoning. Avoid very hot sausages so as not to overwhelm the parsnips. It is cottage food, nothing refined, but simple and good. It's most welcome in cold weather, when garden parsnips reach their peak of flavor. (Don't try harvesting in a really hard freeze, however; the long, breakable roots are next to impossible to get out of the frozen ground.) Fennel can be substituted for all or part of the parsnips.

3 medium parsnips

4 medium leeks, with an inch of green

1 pound Italian-style sausage, bulk or link, in bite-sized patties or slices

3 tablespoons minced parsley

2 tablespoons butter

2 tablespoons flour

1 cup milk

salt and pepper

½ teaspoon paprika

Preheat oven to 350°F. Peel parsnips and steam until nearly tender. Cooking time will vary with size. Slice in half lengthwise and remove core if necessary. Slice parsnip halves into 1-inch sections. Slice trimmed leeks into 2-inch sections.

Cook sausage over low heat in a heavy skillet. Drain off all except 2 tablespoons fat. Add parsnips, leeks, and parsley and sauté until vegetables are soft.

Meanwhile, melt butter in a small saucepan, add flour, and cook over medium heat, stirring constantly, for 3 minutes. Slowly add milk. Bring mixture to the boiling point, still stirring, and then reduce heat to a simmer. Add salt and pepper and cook gently until sauce thickens.

Put vegetable and sausage mixture into a casserole, pour sauce over, and sprinkle with paprika. Bake 30 minutes.

SERVES 4 OR 5.

RED CABBAGE AND CHESTNUTS

This dish is from Limoges in central France. The chestnuts soak up the rich blend of flavors during a slow cooking.

20 fresh chestnuts

¼ pound lean bacon or smoked sausage, diced

2 pounds red cabbage, shredded coarsely

3 cups beef stock

salt and pepper

Preheat oven to 375°F. Cut an X in each chestnut shell and simmer for 10 to 15 minutes in a covered saucepan. Remove from heat, drain, and peel. Chop roughly. Stew bacon or sausage in a small skillet, pouring off excess fat. Place cabbage and bacon or sausage in a large ovenproof casserole, add stock and chestnuts, and season to taste with salt and pepper. Stir gently, cover, and cook until tender, about 1½ hours.

SERVES 4 TO 6.

POT ROAST WITH HAZELNUT BARLEY

A version of this hearty dinner was the winner in a Washington State contest for beef recipes. One food writer at the time sniffed that it just wasn't very nouvelle, but the proof is in the eating. Tender meat, a tangy sauce, and a chewy barley-nut mixture make a good meal with a minimum of fuss.

1 tablespoon olive oil

3- to 4-pound boneless chuck or other lean roast

2 medium onions, chopped fine

2 cloves garlic, chopped

2 tablespoons Dijon mustard

1 teaspoon fresh tarragon or ½ teaspoon dried

2 canned tomatoes, drained and chopped

salt and pepper

2 tablespoons butter

½ cup finely chopped hazelnuts

3 cups water

1 teaspoon salt

1 teaspoon Worcestershire sauce

1½ cups pearl barley

Heat olive oil in a heavy pan. Brown roast over medium heat. Add onion and garlic and cook until they begin to soften. Add mustard, tarragon, tomatoes, salt, and pepper. Cover pan, lower heat, and simmer until roast is tender, 1½ to 2 hours. You don't need any other liquid.

During the last 40 minutes of cooking, melt butter in a heavy saucepan. Add hazelnuts and cook over medium-high heat until they are crisp and brown. Add water, salt, Worcestershire sauce, and barley. Cover and steam over low heat until water is absorbed, about 30 minutes.

Remove meat, slice, and serve with barley and pan juices.

SERVES 4.

BEEF STEW WITH HORSERADISH SAUCE

A Russian dish for a cold day. Prepared horseradish is OK, but fresh grated is better.

¼ cup oil

3 pounds stew beef, cut into 1½-inch cubes

2 onions, chopped fine

4 cloves garlic, crushed

2 carrots, chopped fine

2 cups beef broth

2 cups dry white wine

2 bay leaves

2 tablespoons butter

3 tablespoons flour

½ cup grated horseradish, or more to taste

2 tablespoons Dijon mustard

¼ cup sour cream

salt and pepper

parsley

Melt oil in large, heavy saucepan or Dutch oven. Brown beef on all sides; remove from pan and keep warm. Add onions, garlic, and carrots to saucepan and sauté about 15 minutes over medium-low heat. Smooth vegetables into an even layer over the bottom of the pan and place browned meat on top. Pour broth and wine over meat, add bay leaves, and cover. Simmer 1½ hours until meat is tender. (The dish can be made in advance up to this point.)

Strain off broth, reserving meat and vegetables. Return broth to saucepan and cook at medium-high until reduced to 2 cups.

In a medium pan, make a roux of butter and flour. Stir in broth and cook until thickened. Add horseradish and mustard, stirring well. Gradually add sour cream and heat gently. Do not allow sauce to boil. Check for seasoning, adding more horseradish if you want.

Pour sauce over meat and vegetables in Dutch oven and warm through.

SERVES 6.

BEEF WITH CAULIFLOWER

Beef curries are rare because Hindus are vegetarians and Moslem cuisines focus on lamb and chicken. This one is from the Portuguese Christian community of Goa, on the west coast of India. It makes good use of less-than-tender steak.

1 pound round steak or rib steak

1 medium cauliflower, broken into florets

juice of 1 lemon

1 teaspoon salt

1 teaspoon black pepper

3 tablespoons ghee (see page 218) or light cooking oil

1 large onion, sliced thin

2 cloves garlic, sliced thin

2-inch piece fresh ginger, sliced

1½ teaspoons chili powder

1 teaspoon ground turmeric

1 teaspoon ground cumin

½ cup yogurt

beef stock

2 teaspoons *garam masala* (see next page) or curry powder

1 tablespoon fresh cilantro

Trim fat from beef, pound to tenderize, and cut into strips ½ inch wide. Sprinkle with lemon juice, salt, and black pepper. Marinate, covered, for at least 2 hours. Drain beef, saving marinade. Heat ghee or oil and sauté beef until it colors. Remove from pan and set aside. Add onion and garlic and sauté until soft. Add fresh ginger, chili powder, turmeric, and cumin and cook another 2 minutes.

Spoon in yogurt and cook 3 or 4 minutes. Add cauliflower florets and stir to coat. Add enough beef stock to the marinade to make 1½ cups. Return beef to pan and cook over low heat, covered, until cauliflower is barely tender, about 10 to 12 minutes. Stir in *garam masala* or curry powder, sprinkle cilantro on top, and simmer another 5 minutes.

SERVES 4.

GARAM MASALA

A ubiquitous spice mixture in Indian cooking, garam masala *is varied to suit the dish—sometimes a powder, sometimes a paste. You may find it in Indian specialty shops. It is not the same as commercial curry powder, and it is less likely than curry powder to overwhelm a simple vegetable curry. If you use curry powder in recipes that call for* garam masala, *you might want to cut back on any additional cumin, turmeric, or chili powder.*

The three basic ingredients of *garam masala* are cinnamon sticks, cardamom pods, and cloves, in equal weights.

Spread them on a baking sheet or pie shell and bake about 30 minutes at 200°F. Don't let them scorch. Remove from the oven, shell the cardamom and discard the pods, break the cinnamon sticks, and pulverize the spices in a blender (unless you want true village authenticity, in which case you will grind them with a mortar and pestle). Other common additions are mace, coriander seeds, cumin, and black pepper. Dry *garam masala* keeps for months at room temperature provided the container is tightly closed.

STEW WITH PUMPKIN

The mint helps give this simple stew a nice fresh taste. Cooking time will vary with the type and age of squash. You want the squash to be soft but not mushy. Serve over rice or with a pilaf on the side.

1 pound peeled pumpkin or other winter squash

1 pound beef or pork stew meat

4 cups hot water

salt

3 garlic cloves, minced

1 cup canned tomatoes, drained and chopped

1 tablespoon tomato paste

2 tablespoons lemon juice

1 tablespoon chopped fresh mint leaves or 2 teaspoons dried

Cut pumpkin into 1-inch cubes and set aside. Combine meat, water, and salt in a large pot. Bring to a boil and cook for 2 minutes, removing any scum that rises. Add garlic, tomatoes, tomato paste, and lemon juice. Lower heat and simmer, covered, for 1 hour. Add pumpkin and cook, covered, until pumpkin is soft, about 45 minutes. Stir in mint leaves just before serving.

SERVES 4.

GOBO WRAPPED WITH BEEF

This traditional Japanese dish uses the same cross-grain cut of beef as teriyaki, and the marinade is similar. You need a very sharp knife.

¾ pound very lean boneless beef

¼ cup soy sauce

¼ cup mirin or sweet sherry

¾ pound gobo

4 cups water

1 tablespoon vinegar

Cut beef into thin slices across the grain. Mix soy and mirin or sherry in a small saucepan and heat until warm. Remove from heat; add beef and let stand at least 30 minutes. Scrub and peel gobo, cut into 5-inch lengths, and julienne. Bring water and vinegar to boil, add gobo, cover, reduce heat, and cook until just tender (about 5 minutes). Drain and cool enough to handle.

Holding 4 or 5 gobo strips in a bundle, wrap a beef strip spirally around bundle, covering the gobo. Use a second, overlapping strip if necessary. Stretch meat slightly as you go. Squeeze bundle to press meat firmly to gobo and then return to marinade.

When all bundles are made, remove from marinade and broil or grill. Cook, turning as needed, until lightly browned, 3 or 4 minutes. Cut each bundle into bite-sized pieces.

SERVES 3 OR 4 AS A MAIN COURSE OR 8 AS AN APPETIZER.

BEEF WITH CARDOONS AND MUSHROOMS

This is inspired by a lamb and cardoon dish from the Abruzzi and Molise regions of southern Italy. It was an instant favorite at our house. You can substitute celery for all or part of the cardoons, but it won't be quite the same. Lamb and fennel also are cooked together in this style.

½ cup olive oil, divided

3 pounds round steak, trimmed and cut into serving pieces

salt and pepper

2 pounds cardoons

3 anchovy fillets *or* 2 tablespoons fermented fish sauce

1 onion, chopped

2 cups quartered mushrooms

½ cup dry white wine

Heat ¼ cup of the olive oil in a large, deep skillet with a cover. Add beef, reduce heat to simmer, and season with salt and pepper. Cover and cook for an hour. (The long cooking time makes me suspect that Abruzzians sometimes use mutton in this dish. It's a good method for my very lean, homegrown beef, but you might want to reduce the cooking time if your beef is young and tender.)

Remove leaves and strings from cardoons and cut into 1-inch pieces. Cook 5 minutes in boiling water, remove from heat, and drain. In another skillet, heat remaining ¼ cup olive oil. Add anchovies (if used), onion, and mushrooms and sauté 10 minutes.

Add vegetable mixture to beef. Stir in wine and fish sauce (if used) and cook another 5 minutes. Check seasoning and serve with polenta or rice.

SERVES 6.

VIETNAMESE BEEF WITH LEEKS

The marinade does wonders for a tough cut of beef. Heavy scissors work much better than a knife for trimming the fat and membrane from an undistinguished steak.

1 tablespoon soy sauce

1 tablespoon plus 1 teaspoon fermented fish sauce

1 teaspoon cornstarch

½ teaspoon honey

1 green onion, chopped, or 2 tablespoons chopped chives

1 pound rib steak, trimmed and cut into stir-fry pieces

2 tablespoons light oil

3 or 4 medium leeks, with a little green, cut into 1-inch pieces

1 tablespoon chopped cilantro (optional)

Combine soy sauce, 1 tablespoon of the fish sauce, cornstarch, honey, and green onion or chives in shallow bowl. Add beef and marinate for about an hour. Heat oil in a heavy skillet or wok. Drain meat, add to oil, and cook for 5 minutes over high heat, stirring constantly. Add leeks and the remaining teaspoon of fish sauce and cook briefly. Leeks should still be crunchy. Sprinkle with cilantro (if used) and serve hot.

SERVES 4.

CHICKEN RICE PIE

Older cookbooks feature recipes for the tough meat and unparalleled flavor of old hens from the backyard flock. This meal starts with a 19th-century recipe from Helen Linsenmayer's fine book Cooking Plain *and brightens the taste with sorrel and Parmesan cheese. The tastier the chicken, the better the meal. Sorrel quickly turns into an unappetizing mush when sautéed, so it is added to the casserole uncooked.*

1 cup dry white wine

1 bay leaf

4 shallots or 1 medium onion, quartered

salt and pepper

1 stewing hen, 4 to 5 pounds

1½ cups rice

4 eggs

¾ cup milk

½ cup grated Parmesan cheese

2 cups chopped sorrel leaves

Put wine, bay leaf, shallots or onion, salt, and pepper into a soup kettle. Add chicken and water to cover. Bring to a boil, reduce heat, and simmer until tender, 1 to 3 hours, depending on age of chicken. Remove chicken, skin it, and take meat off the bones.

Strain broth and pour 4 cups into a large saucepan. (Any remaining liquid can be saved for another use.) Bring broth to a boil, add rice, and reduce heat. Cook, covered, until rice is done, about 30 minutes. Remove from heat and let cool slightly.

Beat eggs in a medium bowl with milk and Parmesan cheese and stir mixture into rice.

Layer rice mixture, chicken, and sorrel in a large casserole, beginning and ending with rice. Bake, uncovered, at 350°F for 30 minutes or until a tester inserted in the center comes out clean.

SERVES 6.

SOOKE HARBOUR HOUSE OYSTERS WITH CARROT SAUCE

This unusual sauce treats good oysters with respect, complementing rather than overwhelming them. Gordon Cowen, a chef at Sooke Harbour House near Victoria, British Columbia, suggests substituting butternut squash for all or part of the carrot for a variation in taste. Golden mantle oysters are raised in British Columbia. They are stronger tasting than the more common Pacific oyster.

12 Pacific or golden mantle oysters, broiled or sautéed

2 medium carrots, peeled and sliced thin

½ small onion, sliced thin

2 cloves garlic, chopped

4 tablespoons unsalted butter, divided

2 tablespoons vermouth

¼ cup reduced fish stock

2 tablespoons lemon juice

Italian parsley or other leafy green

Melt 2 tablespoons of the butter in a saucepan, add onion and garlic, and sauté briefly. Add carrots and fish stock and cook, covered, over low heat until carrots are tender. Transfer to blender or food processor and purée. Add vermouth and lemon juice and whisk in remaining 2 tablespoons of butter. Adjust seasoning and thickness to taste.

Pour some sauce onto each of four plates. Place the oysters on the sauce—three per plate. Garnish with Italian parsley or other green and serve.

SERVES 4.

SQUID IN ZIMINO

Cooking squid can be discouraging. First of all, squid are ugly, and if things go wrong in the kitchen they taste like rubber. But well-cooked squid are wonderful. The trick to tenderness is either to cook them very fast—as in Black Bean Sauce Calamari or fritto misto—or for at least 20 minutes, as in this traditional Tuscan dish. "In zimino" refers to cooking with greens.

1 tablespoon olive oil

½ cup chopped onion

1 clove garlic, minced

1 dried red chile pepper, minced

¼ cup chopped parsley

¼ cup chopped chard stem or celery

1 pound squid

1 teaspoon flour

½ cup dried porcini mushrooms, soaked for 30 minutes, drained and chopped, or 1 cup regular mushrooms, or a combination totaling 1 cup

½ cup chopped canned tomatoes

1 pound chard or beet greens

1 cup dry white wine

salt and pepper

First, clean the squid. Here's how: Grab the head and pull it from the mantle. This will bring most of the insides with it. Reach inside the mantle and remove the long piece of cartilage (called the pen) within. Rinse out the mantle. Not all recipes use the tentacles up by the head, but this one does. Chop the creature into ½-inch rings.

Heat olive oil in a saucepan over medium heat. Add onion, garlic, chile pepper, parsley, and chard stem or celery, reduce heat to low, and sauté until onion begins to color. Add squid and cook 10 minutes over medium heat. Sprinkle flour over top and stir it in.

Don't worry if squid is tough at this point. Add mushrooms, tomatoes, greens, and wine. Season with salt and pepper. Cover and simmer 30 minutes.

Uncover and simmer until liquid has evaporated into a coating for squid and vegetables. Serve hot, preferably over polenta.

SERVES 6.

BLACK BEAN CALAMARI

This is from John Kemnitzer, chef at the Yarrow Bay Grill in Kirkland, Washington. It's very, very good, and so healthful that it was reprinted in a magazine for Group Health insurance members. Quick cooking is the key here, so have everything ready in advance. You can buy bottled black bean sauce in most supermarkets if the recipe here sounds too daunting. If you are a straight-from-the-garden purist, you can substitute chard stems or blanched cardoons for the celery.

1 pound squid, cleaned and cut into ½-inch rings

1 cup carrots, julienned

1 cup celery, julienned

½ cup small turnips, julienned (optional)

4 tablespoons cooking oil

1 cup black bean sauce, or more to taste

1 teaspoon black sesame seeds, lightly toasted

1 teaspoon white sesame seeds, lightly toasted

¼ cup sliced green onions

Heat oil in a medium skillet until it just begins to smoke. Add carrots, celery, and turnips (if used) and toss for 30 seconds or until vegetables just begin to cook. Add squid and cook, tossing, until rings start to turn opaque, 1 minute at the most. Add black bean sauce and toss until sauce is hot, about 30 seconds. Garnish with green onions and sesame seeds.

Black bean sauce

I sometimes make a stripped-down sauce out of black beans, garlic, ginger, and soy sauce. It's good, but I admit this one is better. Fermented black beans—as well as the other seasonings for this recipe—are available in Asian markets and some supermarkets. Dry white wine can be substituted for the sake.

3½ cups water, divided

½ cup fermented black beans

1 tablespoon minced garlic

½ cup low-salt soy sauce

4 teaspoons chili-garlic paste

½ tablespoon sesame oil

½ tablespoon minced fresh ginger

½ cup plus 3 tablespoons sake

2 tablespoons sugar

pinch of crushed red chili pepper

¾ teaspoon ground Sichuan pepper

¾ teaspoon Chinese five-spice powder

3 tablespoons cornstarch

Bring 1½ cups water to a boil and add black beans. Simmer 5 minutes. Strain and discard the water. Retain about a quarter of the beans for texture and purée the rest.

Combine the remaining 2 cups water, ½ cup of the sake, and all remaining ingredients except cornstarch in a saucepan and bring to a boil. Add beans and return to boiling. Reduce heat to simmer. Combine cornstarch and remaining 3 tablespoons sake in a small bowl. Add slowly to black beans, whisking to mix thoroughly. Simmer gently for 5 minutes.

MAKES 2 CUPS.
SERVES 4.

BAKED FISH AND CHICORY

Simple pleasures are the best. The top layer of chicory will brown slightly, but that's fine.

2 pounds fillet of sole

2 pounds chicory

salt and pepper

1 tablespoon chopped parsley

1 large clove garlic, minced

½ cup olive oil

Preheat oven to 400°F. Wash and dry sole fillets, cut lengthwise into small strips, and dry again. Tear chicory, wash, and dry carefully.

Arrange chicory and fish in alternate layers in an oiled baking dish, seasoning each layer with salt, pepper, parsley, garlic, and oil. End with a layer of chicory and seasoning. Bake for 35 minutes.

SERVES 6.

SOLE AU VERT

The combination of herbs here is a suggestion, not an order. If you don't use any sorrel, sprinkle fillets with lemon juice before serving.

1 fillet of sole per diner

salt and pepper

¼ cup flour

3 tablespoons butter, divided

1 cup chopped sorrel or spinach

2 tablespoons chopped chives

2 tablespoons chopped parsley

2 teaspoons chopped tarragon

Salt and pepper sole fillets and dust with flour. Heat 2 tablespoons of the butter in skillet and cook fillets, turning to brown lightly on both sides. Add sorrel or spinach, herbs, and the remaining 1 tablespoon butter and simmer until greens are tender but not mushy, 3 or 4 minutes.

SERVES 4.

TEMPURA

Tempura is perfect for the winter garden, allowing you to combine a bit of this and a leaf of that into a harmonious meal. The ingredients must be fresh, but they need not be pretty.

Food writer Jennifer Brennan says that the Japanese acquired the technique for batter-fried food from 16th-century Portuguese traders and that the name derives from the Latin tempora. Russ Rudzinski, co-owner of a pioneer Japanese country-style restaurant in San Francisco, offers a Buddhist monk as an originator and a more poetic etymology: three picture characters—tem, meaning heaven; pu, meaning woman; and ra, meaning silken veil. Therefore, a woman veiled in silk, offering a glimpse of heaven. Anyway, it tastes wonderful and the techniques are simple, although time-consuming and a bit messy.

Another subject of debate is the batter. Brennan emphasizes that it must be absolutely fresh, preferably made in two batches while the cooking is in progress. Rudzinski wants you to make it at least 15 minutes in advance. I'm with him, since the batter is basically the same as fritter batter, which also benefits from a refrigerated rest before cooking. I have had good results with his recipe, which I pass on here. I also have been satisfied with commercial tempura mix. However you do it, the point is to avoid activating the gluten in the flour, so that the batter doesn't get rubbery. I go into all this detail on the great tempura debate to emphasize the dangers of blindly following any expert. What works in your kitchen is the right way to do it.

You need to be attentive while frying, so prepare all the vegetables and seafood in advance.

Just one more thing: Japanese cooks also make a related dish, abura yaki, which uses the same oil but no batter. Use firm vegetables and lean meat, usually beef, all sliced about ¼ inch thick. Fry for a few minutes in the hot oil and serve with a dipping sauce.

Vegetables and seafood

broccoli florets

cauliflower florets

spinach leaves, washed and dried

sweet potatoes, peeled and sliced about ¼ inch thick

small cubes of pumpkin or other winter squash

mushrooms, sliced lengthwise

carrots, peeled and sliced on the diagonal

celery, in 1-inch chunks

shrimp, prawns, or chunks of firm white fish

vegetable oil for frying

Batter for 4

2¼ cups all-purpose flour, divided

½ teaspoon baking powder

2 eggs

2 cups ice water

Mix 2 cups of the flour with all remaining ingredients. The mixture should be the consistency of whipping cream; a few lumps are OK. Let stand 15 minutes before use. Put remaining ¼ cup flour in a small, shallow bowl.

Dipping sauce

1 cup chicken stock or *dashi* (Japanese fish stock, available in powdered form)

¼ cup sugar

½ cup soy sauce

2 tablespoons mirin or sherry

1 tablespoon grated daikon (optional)

Combine all dipping ingredients and stir until sugar is dissolved.

Shell shrimp and prawns, leaving tails attached. Clean and devein them. Score each shrimp several times across its underside to reduce curling. Butterfly large prawns open to increase cooking surface. Dry shrimp and prawns thoroughly; the batter won't stick on a wet surface.

Pour oil into a wok, deep-fat fryer, or electric frying pan. (The oil can be strained, refrigerated, and reused.) The amount of oil depends on the size of your container, but the greater the volume, the easier it is to maintain the proper temperature. Four cups is a reasonable amount for a standard wok. Heat oil to between 350° and 375°F. If you don't have a deep-fat thermometer, test with a spoonful of batter. It should drop to the bottom of the fryer and then rise almost immediately to the surface. If the batter doesn't drop, the oil is too hot. If it doesn't rise, the oil is too cold.

Starting with vegetables and ending with seafood, roll each piece in the small bowl of flour and then dip into the batter. Drain off the surplus batter, and then drop the pieces gently into the oil. Fry for 2 to 3 minutes, remove, and drain on paper towels. Do not crowd the items as they fry. They must be able to float on the surface, and the temperature must not drop below 350°. When pieces are drained, place them on a heated serving plate and keep warm until everything is cooked. Serve immediately with small bowls of dipping sauce.

PRAWN CURRY

This dish is from Bangladesh, and it's wonderful. Unlike some spicy prawn dishes, in this one you still can taste the seafood. Mint Chutney (see page 219) makes an excellent condiment.

½ pound prawns

2 pounds fresh spinach or one 12-ounce box frozen spinach

3 tablespoons ghee (see page 218) or light oil

1 medium onion, sliced

1 clove garlic, chopped

2 inches cinnamon stick

1 teaspoon ground cumin

½ teaspoon turmeric

1 teaspoon ground coriander seeds

2 teaspoons chili powder

1 teaspoon black pepper

½ cup tomato paste

1 teaspoon honey

1 teaspoon salt

1 teaspoon *garam masala* (see page 141) or ½ teaspoon curry powder

Peel prawns. If spinach is fresh, chop leaves coarsely and steam for 5 minutes. Remove from heat and drain. If spinach is frozen, thaw partially and chop into 1-inch cubes. Heat oil in a large saucepan or skillet. Sauté onion and garlic until onion starts to soften. Add cinnamon, cumin, turmeric, coriander, chili powder, and black pepper. Sauté 2 minutes.

Add tomato purée and honey and cook another minute, mixing well. Add spinach and salt and stir well to coat spinach with tomato-spice mixture. Add prawns. Cook gently, turning prawns so they color on both sides. When prawns are pink, add *garam masala* or curry powder and cook another 5 minutes. The curry should be fairly dry, not soupy.

SERVES 4.

MOULES MARINIÈRE

Not so many years ago, clam diggers and oyster gatherers would walk right by succulent mussel beds in search of bigger game. Now mussels are so popular that they are available commercially. Winter is a fine time for them because the red-tide danger is at its lowest point. If you gather your own, pick only tightly closed specimens and avoid highly polluted waterways.

Cilantro makes a nice change from parsley in this recipe. You could change the name to mejillones a la marinera *so as not to offend the French.*

50 mussels

¼ cup butter

2 cloves garlic, chopped

4 tablespoons chopped shallots

3 leeks (white part only), chopped

1 bay leaf

salt and pepper

¾ cup dry white wine

chopped parsley or cilantro

Scrub mussels and remove beards. Melt butter in soup kettle. Add garlic and shallots and cook gently for 1 minute. Add leeks and bay leaf and cook until vegetables are limp.

Add mussels, salt, pepper, and white wine. Cover and cook gently until mussels open. Discard any that don't.

Remove mussels and divide into bowls. Strain broth, return it to the kettle, and cook without boiling for 2 or 3 minutes. Pour over mussels, garnish with parsley or cilantro, and serve.

SERVES 4.

BAGNA CAUDA

Bagna cauda *("hot bath") is a traditional northern Italian winter dish, featuring the small, sweet cardoons of the Piedmont region. The vegetables and sauce can be prepared ahead of time, allowing instant gratification after a day out in the cold. Keep cardoon slices in acidulated water until serving time so they don't turn brown. Use a candle warmer or a fondue setup to keep the sauce hot at the table.*

1 cup olive oil

4 tablespoons butter

3 teaspoons finely chopped garlic

10 to 12 anchovy fillets (one small can), chopped fine

fresh raw vegetables suitable for dipping, such as broccoli, sliced carrots, radishes, spinach leaves, young kale, kohlrabi, celeriac, and blanched cardoons

Heat oil and butter until mixture foams slightly. Add garlic and sauté over low heat for about 3 minutes. Add anchovies and cook gently until they dissolve into a paste. Keep sauce hot at the table and stir occasionally to keep the anchovies blended. Provide lots of bread for dipping.

SERVES 4.

SIDE DISHES

TERIYAKI BEETS

Most people think they hate beets, but it's entirely possible they only hate sweet-and-sour Harvard beets, which are indeed an outrage. Beets are not subtle vegetables, but they can be delicious. The soy sauce and ginger in this dish are excellent complements to the earthy sweetness of the beets. You could broil them alongside some nice halibut and serve with rice and a green salad or Sprout Salad (page 102).

12 small unpeeled beets

4 tablespoons butter

2 tablespoons honey

1 tablespoon finely chopped fresh ginger

1 tablespoon soy sauce

Boil or steam beets until almost tender. Time will vary with size and age of beets. Rinse in cold water, peel, and cut into halves. In a small saucepan, combine butter, honey, ginger, and soy sauce and heat until butter and honey are melted. Brush some of the sauce over beets and place on a heated broiler pan. Broil 8 or 10 minutes or until tender, basting frequently. Transfer to serving dish and pour remaining sauce over.

SERVES 4 TO 6.

GINGERED BEETS AND BRUSSELS SPROUTS

Really fresh Brussels sprouts are important here.

1 pound Brussels sprouts (about 3 cups), trimmed

2 medium beets, boiled, baked, or steamed

2 tablespoons butter

2 teaspoons fresh grated ginger

2 tablespoons lemon juice

salt and pepper

Cut an X in the stem of each Brussels sprout and steam over boiling water until nearly tender, 5 to 7 minutes. Remove from heat. Peel and slice beets. Cut sprouts in half if they are really large. Heat butter in a medium skillet or saucepan, add sprouts, beets, and ginger, and sauté until vegetables are tender. Add lemon juice, salt, and pepper and cook very gently another 2 or 3 minutes.

SERVES 4.

FRIED BROCCOLI STEMS

Broccoli stems will keep for several days in the refrigerator. Deep-fry them, serve with soy sauce, and you have an approximation of tempura. Substitute ketchup and you can sneak healthy greens into small children.

stems from one large head of broccoli

¾ cup flour

¼ cup cornstarch

1½ teaspoons baking powder

½ teaspoon salt

¾ cup water

oil for frying

Peel broccoli stems and slice on a slight diagonal into ¼-inch rounds. Steam until almost tender, about 5 minutes, plunge into cold water, and drain. Pat dry so batter will stick.

Beat together flour, cornstarch, baking powder, salt, and water to make a batter. Heat oil in wok or deep fryer. When it reaches 375°F, dip out a spoonful of oil and stir into the batter. If you don't have a thermometer, check with a sample of battered broccoli. It should sink to the bottom and then rise immediately.

Using tongs, dip broccoli in batter, let excess drip off, and put the pieces into the oil about 5 at a time. When slices are browned and puffy, remove with a slotted spoon and drain on paper towels.

SERVES 3 OR 4.

BROCCOLI ROMEO

Romeo Conca, a terrific cook, uses this treatment to get the most flavor and nutrition out of homegrown broccoli or kale. Good cooking doesn't come any simpler than this. I quote his instructions verbatim:

If there is no danger of cabbage worms or aphids, pick directly into a saucepan, cover the greens with water, and then drain off all the water. If there is a concern for bugs, cover with well-salted water and observe carefully. Again drain completely. The small amount of water trapped in the greens is all that's needed. Add a clove, or two if small, of garlic, some salt, a grind of pepper, and a liberal drizzle of olive oil, cover with a well-fitting lid, and cook on low heat. Depending on quantities, 10 or 15 minutes is enough. This method of cooking retains the flavor—no liquid to drain off—and so both broccoli and kale have a somewhat more pronounced flavor.

BROCCOLI LEEK PURÉE

This fresh-tasting purée, flecked with light and dark green, is good with roast poultry. The slight sweetness of the leeks complements the broccoli, which is not cooked, only blanched. To make it into a main dish, put the purée into a casserole, place sautéed chicken breasts or sautéed fish fillets on top, and bake 10 minutes at 350°F.

1 bunch broccoli (about 3 cups florets)

4 or 5 medium leeks

½ cup cottage cheese

3 tablespoons butter

salt and pepper

freshly grated nutmeg

Steam broccoli florets over boiling water for 3 minutes. Drain, submerge in cold water, and drain again when broccoli is cool. Don't let broccoli cook until it is soft—it spoils the dish.

Trim leeks, cut into ½-inch pieces, and wash. Boil in salted water until tender but not mushy, about 8 minutes. Drain, rinse briefly in cold water, and press out liquid. Purée broccoli and leeks together with cottage cheese. Melt butter and add to purée. Season to taste with salt, pepper, and nutmeg.

SERVES 4.

SAUTÉ OF BROCCOLI AND TURNIPS

Simple and attractive, this quick dish rises several culinary notches when you have fresh young turnips. Steam the vegetables separately so that you can monitor their crispness closely. They need to keep a little crunch.

1 pound broccoli (about 3 cups), peeled and trimmed

¾ pound (5 or 6) small turnips, peeled and cut into ¾-inch wedges

2 tablespoons butter

2 tablespoons oil

½ teaspoon sugar

salt and pepper

Cut florets from broccoli stems. Cut stems into ¼-inch diagonals. Steam stems 4 minutes over boiling water. Add florets and cook another 3 or 4 minutes, until barely tender. Remove broccoli and let it cool.

Put turnips in steamer and cook until barely tender, about 5 minutes. Remove from heat.

Melt butter and oil in large, heavy skillet over medium–high heat. Add turnips and sugar and stir until lightly browned. Add broccoli and toss until vegetables are heated through. Season with salt and pepper.

SERVES 4.

BRUSSELS SPROUTS IN LEMON CURRY SAUCE

Many Indian dishes are so distinctively flavored that they clash with any other style of cooking, but these crisp sprouts and their tangy sauce go well with a plain roast chicken or even a meatloaf. You will need rice to soak up the sauce. Frozen sprouts are not as good, but they are better than really tired fresh ones. You also can substitute lightly steamed sliced cabbage or kohlrabi.

1½ pounds fresh or 1 pound frozen Brussels sprouts

3 tablespoons ghee (see page 218) or light cooking oil

1 onion, sliced thin

3 cloves garlic, sliced thin

1 teaspoon ground turmeric

1½ teaspoons chili powder

2 inches whole cinnamon or 1 teaspoon ground

2 teaspoons poppy seeds

1 teaspoon ground cumin

1 teaspoon ground coriander seeds

1 cup yogurt

juice of 1 lemon

salt and pepper

2 tablespoons honey

2 tablespoons chopped cilantro (optional)

Preheat oven to 400°F. Wash and trim fresh Brussels sprouts or thaw frozen ones. Cut a slash in the base of each sprout and arrange sprouts in one layer in a large covered casserole or baking dish. Heat ghee or oil in a medium saucepan. Add onion and garlic and sauté gently until soft; don't let them burn. Add turmeric, chili powder, cinnamon, poppy seed, and cumin and cook, stirring, for 2 to 3 minutes. Stir in cilantro.

Transfer mixture to blender. Add yogurt, honey, and lemon juice and blend. Add salt and pepper to taste and blend again. Pour mixture over sprouts. Bake, covered, for 15 to 20 minutes. Remove cover, mix gently so that sprouts are well covered with sauce, and cook uncovered until sprouts are done, maybe another 10 minutes. Don't overcook them. Sprinkle with cilantro (if used) and serve.

SERVES 4.

BRUSSELS SPROUTS IN CELERY SAUCE

This company dish is one of Judy Gorman's many innovative vegetable creations. It is delicious and very attractive, with bright green sprouts peeking out of the pale green sauce.

1 pound Brussels sprouts

8 ribs celery

½ cup water

3 tablespoons butter

1 tablespoon flour

1 cup half-and-half

salt and pepper

nutmeg

Preheat oven to 350°F. Boil or steam sprouts until barely tender. Drain, plunge briefly into cold water, shake off excess moisture, and transfer to a shallow buttered baking dish. Remove strings from celery and slice the ribs thin. Bring water to boil in a medium saucepan, add celery, and cook over medium heat until tender, about 10 minutes. Purée celery and cooking water, return to saucepan, and cook over low heat until reduced by half.

While celery is reducing, melt butter in a small saucepan, sprinkle on flour, and stir over medium heat until mixture foams. Whisk in half-and-half and continue stirring until bubbly and slightly thickened. Whisk in celery mixture. Season with salt, pepper, and nutmeg.

Pour celery sauce over sprouts and toss to coat. Bake 20 minutes.

SERVES 4.

CABBAGE WITH COCONUT

This South Indian dish can also be made with savoy or Chinese cabbage. It can be very hot, depending on the type and amount of chiles. Unsweetened coconut is available at natural food stores and Asian and Indian markets.

½ medium cabbage, sliced into thin ribbons

3 tablespoons vegetable oil

1 large onion, sliced thin

2 cloves garlic, sliced

4 hot green chiles (or fewer, according to taste), seeded and chopped

2-inch piece of fresh ginger, sliced

1 teaspoon salt

1 tablespoon unsweetened dried coconut

Steam cabbage about 5 minutes. It should still be crunchy. Remove from heat and drain. Do not dry. Heat oil in a skillet or large saucepan. Add onion, garlic, and ginger and sauté until onion begins to soften. Add chopped chiles and sauté about 2 minutes. Add cabbage, reduce heat, and mix thoroughly. Add salt and coconut and continue to cook, stirring, until coconut is moist and cabbage is heated through. It should not be completely soft. Serve warm.

SERVES 4.

KIM CHEE

Kim chee is a generic name for a hot fermented pickle that is ubiquitous in Korea —where it accompanies every meal—and common in Japan. It can be made with vegetables ranging from spinach to cucumber, but it most commonly contains nappa cabbage and daikon and serves as a way to preserve these vegetables in quantity through the winter. The taste and smell are unforgettable. I love it, not only with Asian food but with grilled cheese sandwiches and in Russian shchi soup (see page 59). There are a number of commercial brands with varying textures and firepower. It's also simple to make at home.

1 medium head nappa cabbage (about 2 pounds), in bite-sized chunks

2 tablespoons plus 1 teaspoon salt, divided

1 cup julienned daikon or kohlrabi (optional)

2 green onions or small leeks, chopped

3 cloves garlic, minced

1 to 2 teaspoons chopped hot red pepper or cayenne

Put cabbage in a large bowl. Sprinkle with 2 tablespoons of the salt and mix. Cover and let stand at room temperature until cabbage wilts to about half its original volume. This will take about 3 hours. Rinse well, drain, and return to bowl along with daikon or kohlrabi (if used), green onions or leeks, garlic, pepper, and the remaining teaspoon of salt. Mix well, pack into a quart jar, cover lightly, and let stand at room temperature until it is fermented to your taste. This will take from 1 to 4 days, depending on the temperature and your preference. *Do not* use a tight cover during fermentation. Strong forces are at work here, and you risk an eruption when the pressure is released. You can and should keep kim chee tightly covered once it's in the refrigerator, however, unless you want the rest of your groceries to smell peculiar.

Some stores also carry a bottled seasoning base for kim chee. One brand name is Momoya (imported from Japan), and it produces excellent kim chee. Just prepare the vegetables as described above, omitting the garlic and red pepper, and pour the bottled mixture on before fermentation.

MAKES ABOUT 3½ CUPS

STEWED CARDOONS

This dish presents the unadorned flavor of cardoons. Once cooked, they can be sprinkled with a cup of grated cheese and run under the broiler, or covered with cream sauce and some bread crumbs and baked 20 minutes at 400°F.

4 pounds cardoons (about 8 big stalks)

3 tablespoons lemon juice

3 tablespoons olive oil

2 cups water

2 cloves garlic, sliced

2 tablespoons chopped parsley

salt and pepper

Remove any tough strings and slice cardoons into ½-inch pieces. Add lemon juice to a bowl of cold water, add cardoons, and let stand for 15 minutes. Drain and cook about 20 minutes in 1 inch of lightly salted water. Drain again and put in medium skillet with 2 cups water, olive oil, garlic, parsley, salt, and pepper. Cook, covered, at low heat for 30 minutes. Remove cover and continue simmering until liquid is evaporated.

SERVES 6.

CARDOONS PELLEGRINI

Angelo Pellegrini has been speaking out on behalf of cardoons for decades. Rather than depend on the whims of the marketplace, he raises his own cardoons in his Seattle garden. He also recommends this recipe for savoy cabbage, collards, kale, and other strong-flavored greens.

1 pound cardoons

2 ounces lean salt pork, minced and pounded to a paste

2 tablespoons olive oil

2 teaspoons butter

3 shallots or 1 small onion, minced

2 cloves garlic

1 tablespoon chopped celery leaves

⅓ cup tomato sauce

⅓ cup beef or chicken stock

3 tablespoons lemon juice

Trim and slice cardoons into 2-inch pieces and blanch 3 or 4 minutes in boiling salted water. Remove and drain. (You can save the cooking water for soup.) Melt salt pork, olive oil, and butter in a skillet. Add shallots or onion, garlic, and celery leaves and sauté gently, watching carefully so mixture does not brown. Add tomato sauce, stock, and lemon juice. Simmer a few minutes until mixture is well blended. Add cardoons, cover, and cook until tender.

SERVES 4.

Cardoons à la Lyonnaise

You can serve cardoons with a simple cream sauce, but the delicate artichoke flavor goes especially well with the bit of lemon and Gruyère in this dish.

1 pound slender cardoons

juice of 1 lemon, divided

2 tablespoons olive oil

1 tablespoon butter

1 tablespoon flour

1 cup vegetable stock

1 cup dry white wine

½ cup Gruyère cheese, grated

salt and pepper

Preheat oven to 425°F. Cut cardoons into bite-sized pieces and sprinkle with half the lemon juice. Simmer about 30 minutes in a medium saucepan with just enough water to cover. Remove cardoons from heat, drain, and sauté in olive oil over medium heat until golden brown. Meanwhile, heat stock gently and add wine.

Melt butter in small saucepan. Add flour, stirring to mix thoroughly. Gradually add stock and wine mixture, stirring constantly. Cook gently until mixture thickens, simmer 5 more minutes, and remove from heat. Stir in cheese and remaining lemon juice.

Put cardoons in shallow casserole. Pour sauce over and bake, uncovered, 10 to 15 minutes.

SERVES 4.

CARROTS WITH CASHEWS

This dish is a good choice for new-comers to East Indian cooking, since it is flavorful without being very hot. Omit the chili powder if you are substituting curry powder for the garam masala.

½ cup light vegetable oil or ghee (see page 218)

1 pound carrots (3 or 4 medium), sliced on the diagonal, about ¼ inch thick

1 large onion, sliced

2-inch piece fresh ginger, sliced thin

1 teaspoon *garam masala* (see page 141)

1 teaspoon chili powder

2 teaspoons flour

½ pound (1½ cups) cashew nuts

½ cup chicken or vegetable stock

salt to taste

½ cup canned tomatoes, seeded, drained, and chopped

Heat oil or ghee and sauté carrots and onion for 2 minutes. Add sliced ginger, *garam masala*, and chili powder. Cook, stirring, until vegetables are coated. Add flour and continue to stir. As mixture thickens, add cashews, stock, and salt. Bring to a boil; lower heat and simmer, covered, until carrots are tender but not mushy. Time will depend on the carrots —start checking after 10 minutes.

Add tomatoes and cook gently another 5 or 6 minutes. The sauce should be a thick coating on the carrots. If it is still very liquid, raise heat and boil briskly until excess liquid has evaporated.

SERVES 4.

CARROT CURRY

This falls somewhere between a chutney and a curry, and it goes well with Indian Spinach with Potatoes (page 124). The spices keep the carrots and fruit from being insipidly sweet. Ghee is a form of clarified butter much used in India. Removing the milk solids makes it possible to store butter without refrigeration, and the milder flavor lets the other seasonings shine through. If you don't have ghee, I think a light vegetable oil makes a better substitute than regular butter.

4 to 5 cups peeled and sliced carrots

1 cup fresh orange juice

$\frac{1}{2}$ cup water

1 teaspoon salt

4 tablespoons ghee (see page 218) or light oil

4 cardamom pods, seeded, or $\frac{1}{2}$ teaspoon ground cardamom

$1\frac{1}{2}$ teaspoons turmeric

$1\frac{1}{2}$ teaspoons mustard seeds

4 cloves

$\frac{1}{4}$ teaspoon cayenne

$\frac{1}{2}$ teaspoon curry powder

1 banana, sliced thin

2 to 3 tablespoons raisins

Simmer carrots with orange juice, salt, and water for about 5 minutes. Remove from heat but do not drain. Heat ghee or oil in skillet and add spices. Sauté a few minutes, using a spatula to prevent sticking. Add carrots with their liquid, raisins, and banana. Simmer slowly about half an hour, until sauce is thick. Avoid unnecessary stirring so the banana slices don't disintegrate.

SERVES 4 TO 6.

CARROT RISOTTO

This is a good deal lighter than risotto Milanese, and it's delicious. Adding the stock bit by bit helps give a risotto the proper creamy texture.

6 cups chicken stock

5 tablespoons butter, divided

1 medium onion, chopped fine

2½ cups rice, preferably Arborio

1 cup dry white wine

1½ cups finely grated carrots

Parmesan cheese

pinch of nutmeg

salt and pepper

Bring stock to a simmer. Reduce heat to low. Melt 4 tablespoons of the butter in a heavy 3-quart saucepan over medium heat. Sauté onion in butter until pale yellow. Add rice and mix to coat with butter. Add white wine and cook, stirring, about 5 minutes or until wine is evaporated.

Add enough hot stock to cover rice, about 3 cups. Reduce heat to low and cook, covered, stirring frequently, until stock has been absorbed. Continue cooking 10 minutes, stirring and adding ½ cup stock at a time, making sure stock is absorbed before the next addition. Add carrots and continue stirring and adding stock until rice is tender but still firm to the bite, about 10 minutes. Remove from heat. Stir in remaining tablespoon butter, ½ cup of the Parmesan cheese, nutmeg, salt, and pepper. Serve with additional cheese.

SERVES 8.

CARROT FETTUCCINE

Thin strips of carrot stand in for pasta, with a delicate cream sauce. Judy Gorman's original recipe calls for 1½ cups of heavy cream, but it seems plenty rich to me with half-and-half. Substituting yogurt for ½ cup of the cream lowers the fat content further, but also alters the taste. Use a mild-flavored oil.

1 pound carrots, preferably coreless

3 tablespoons light oil

1½ cups half-and-half

salt and pepper

freshly grated nutmeg

½ cup grated Parmesan cheese

Use a vegetable peeler to make thin strips of carrot. Heat oil in a large skillet. Add carrots and toss to coat evenly. Stir over medium heat for about 1 minute. Add half-and-half and bring mixture to a gentle bubble. Cook uncovered, stirring occasionally, until half-and-half is reduced by half and carrots are tender. Season with salt and pepper and sprinkle with nutmeg. Transfer to a serving plate and sprinkle with Parmesan cheese.

SERVES 4.

GEORGIAN-STYLE CAULIFLOWER

Cauliflower and cilantro are an excellent combination, often found in curries. This dish from the Soviet Republic of Georgia uses the same flavors to different effect, accentuating the sweetness of a really fresh cauliflower.

1 small cauliflower, separated into florets

4 tablespoons butter or light oil

2 small onions, finely chopped

4 tablespoons butter, divided

4 tablespoons minced parsley

2 tablespoons minced cilantro

2 large eggs, beaten

salt and pepper

Steam cauliflower over boiling water for 10 minutes. Remove from heat and drain. Meanwhile, sauté onions in a large pan with 3 tablespoons of the butter or oil until golden. Add the remaining 1 tablespoon of butter or oil and stir in cauliflower, turning florets to coat them well. Cook, covered, for 10 minutes more, until tender.

Stir in parsley, cilantro, and eggs. Toss mixture gently to distribute the egg coating and then cook only until the eggs are done. Season to taste.

SERVES 4.

CELERIAC PURÉES

Celeriac purées well, and its mild, slightly sweet flavor combines nicely with other vegetables. Experimentation will show you which combinations your family likes best. Potatoes are always a good place to start.

Celeriac and potatoes

2½ to 3 pounds celeriac (about 4 medium roots), peeled and cut into ½-inch slices

3 to 4 tablespoons butter, divided

½ teaspoon salt

2 cups warm mashed potatoes

pepper

Put celeriac in saucepan with 2 tablespoons butter, salt, and enough water to barely cover. Bring to boil, cover, and simmer slowly for 25 to 30 minutes or until tender. Uncover and cook until any liquid evaporates.

Purée celeriac and combine with potatoes. Warm briefly, season with pepper to taste, and stir in the remaining butter.

Another classic recipe uses ¾ pound of apples to each pound of celeriac. Cook the celeriac for 20 minutes before adding the peeled, sliced apples. When the apples are tender, purée the mixture. Add milk or cream until you reach the consistency you want, season with salt and pepper to taste, and serve.

SERVES 8.

Celeriac and cheese

4 medium celeriacs, peeled

2 large eggs, separated

½ cup whole milk or half-and-half

salt and pepper

1 cup grated Gruyère or other firm cheese

1 cup plain yogurt

3 tablespoons lemon juice

1 tablespoon chopped fresh parsley

Cook celeriacs in boiling water until tender, about 30 minutes. Drain. Cut into quarters and purée, using as much of the milk or half-and-half as necessary to get the mixture smooth.

Preheat oven to 350°F. Combine purée, egg yolks, remaining milk, salt, and pepper in a mixing bowl. Beat until well blended and stir in cheese. Beat egg whites into soft peaks and fold into the celeriac mixture.

Pour into a large buttered casserole or a 5-by-9-inch loaf pan. There must be enough room for the mixture to rise. Cover and bake until a tester comes out clean, about 30 to 40 minutes.

Allow to cool for 5 minutes and unmold onto a serving plate. Serve with a sauce made of the yogurt, lemon juice, and parsley.

SERVES 6 AS A SIDE DISH OR 4 AS A MAIN DISH.

STUFFED CELERIAC

I thought this dish sounded boring until I tried it. The taste is mild, but the effect is far from dull. You can vary the filling to suit your taste and your larder, but it should not be so strongly flavored as to overpower the celeriac. This recipe also can be made with kohlrabi.

3 medium celeriac roots

4 tablespoons butter, divided

4 shallots, chopped, or ¼ cup chopped onion

1 pound mushrooms, chopped

½ cup finely chopped cooked beef, pork, or chicken

1 tablespoon flour

1 cup milk

Preheat oven to 325°F. Peel celeriacs, cut in half crosswise, and blanch in boiling water. Drain and let cool slightly. Scoop out a hollow in each half. Chop the scoopings fine.

Sauté shallots or onion gently in 3 tablespoons of the butter. Add mushrooms and sauté about 5 minutes. Add beef, pork, or chicken, sprinkle on flour, and mix well. Add chopped celeriac scoopings and milk and heat through.

Fill celeriacs with the stuffing, arrange in an oiled casserole, and dot remaining butter on top. Cover casserole and bake until celeriacs are tender, about 45 minutes.

SERVES 6.

RISOTTO WITH CHESTNUTS

Intriguing and delicious, this contemporary Italian dish goes well with chicken. We like it so much we sometimes have it as a main course.

1 pound fresh chestnuts or ½ pound dried

1 bay leaf

2 medium leeks, white part only, or 1 small onion, minced

4 tablespoons butter, divided

1½ cups rice

3 cups beef or vegetable stock

½ cup half-and-half

¼ cup sliced almonds (optional)

3 tablespoons grated Parmesan cheese

Soak dried chestnuts for 1 hour in lukewarm water. Skip the soaking if you have fresh nuts. Cut an X on the flat side of each shell and simmer with bay leaf for 20 to 30 minutes. Cool, peel, and crumble into a small bowl. Melt 2 tablespoons of the butter in a medium saucepan and sauté leeks or onion until translucent. Add rice and half of the crumbled chestnuts and sauté about 2 minutes. Pour in stock, stirring, and cover pan. Bring to a boil, lower heat, and simmer for 25 minutes or until rice is just cooked. Heat half-and-half in a small pan. Add sliced almonds (if used) and remaining chestnuts and cook over very low heat for 5 minutes. Mash a few of the chestnuts in the half-and-half, stir, and add mixture to rice along with Parmesan cheese and the remaining 2 tablespoons of butter.

SERVES 4.

BRAISED DAIKON

The simple sauce caramelizes slightly and the resulting dish is very appealing. It goes well with a roast, with baked fish, or with Japanese dishes.

1½ pounds fresh daikon, peeled and diced

2 tablespoons light cooking oil

1 teaspoon sugar

1½ tablespoons soy sauce

¼ cup water

Put daikon in a saucepan, cover with water, and bring to a boil. Boil for about 5 minutes, drain, and set aside. Heat a skillet or heavy saucepan, add oil, and stir-fry daikon for 2 minutes. Add sugar and soy sauce. Stir and mix for another minute so that sugar and soy coat daikon. Add water, cover, and bring to boil. Reduce heat to medium-low and cook about 30 minutes or until daikon is tender but not mushy. Stir occasionally to keep daikon coated with sauce. Serve hot.

SERVES 4.

ETHIOPIAN COLLARDS AND COTTAGE CHEESE

Niter kibbeh, *a spiced clarified butter, gives this dish its unique flavor. I had never imagined collards could taste so good. Ethiopian cottage cheese is tarter and drier than the regular American type. If your grocery sells dry cottage cheese, or if you make your own, you can come closer to the authentic taste. Increase the amount of* niter kibbeh *in the first part of the recipe to ½ cup if you are using dry cottage cheese.*

Spiced cheese

12 ounces cottage cheese

⅓ cup *niter kibbeh* (see page 218)

2 garlic cloves, slightly crushed, not chopped

¼ teaspoon ground cardamom

½ teaspoon salt

¼ teaspoon pepper

Mix cottage cheese, the ⅓ cup of *niter kibbeh*, garlic, cardamom, salt, and pepper together and let flavors combine at room temperature for 15 minutes.

Greens

2 pounds collards, chopped, with stems removed

2 tablespoons minced chile pepper

1 tablespoon fresh grated ginger

1 teaspoon minced garlic

½ teaspoon ground cardamom

2 teaspoons minced onion

¼ cup *niter kibbeh*

Steam collards for about 20 minutes (less if the leaves are young and tender). Put collards in a bowl. Add chile pepper, ginger, garlic, cardamom, onion, and the ¼ cup of *niter kibbeh* and mix thoroughly. Remove garlic from cottage cheese. Serve collards and cheese in separate dishes, or spoon greens over cheese in one large bowl.

SERVES 6 TO 8.

ESCAROLE AND RED CABBAGE

The red-violet cabbage and bright green escarole make this an exceptionally beautiful dish, provided you serve it right away. It tastes even better the next day, but the color changes to a uniform and peculiar purple. The smooth leaves of escarole contrast nicely with the cabbage, but the dish also can be made with chicory.

2 tablespoons vegetable oil

2 tablespoons butter

1 head red cabbage, shredded

2 teaspoons caraway seed

1 cup water

1 head escarole or chicory, sliced into shreds

salt and pepper

Heat oil and butter in a large skillet. Add cabbage and toss to coat. Cook, stirring, over medium heat for 1 minute. Add caraway seed, pour in water, and reduce heat. Cover pan and simmer for 10 to 12 minutes or until cabbage is almost tender.

Add escarole or chicory and stir to combine. Increase heat and cook, stirring, until greens are limp and liquid is evaporated. Season with salt and pepper.

SERVES 6.

BRAISED FENNEL

Braising in a little water concentrates the flavor of the fennel. This simple dish is good with broiled fish or pork.

fennel bulbs, sliced thick

1 tablespoon olive oil per bulb

1 garlic clove per bulb, bruised

salt

$\frac{1}{3}$ cup water per bulb

pepper

chopped fennel leaves, for garnish

Heat olive oil in a heavy skillet or saucepan. Add garlic and cook briefly over medium heat. Add lightly salted fennel slices and cook about 10 minutes at medium–low.

Add water, scrape bottom of pan, cover, and cook gently about 20 minutes. Serve with a sprinkling of pepper and chopped fennel leaves.

2 MEDIUM BULBS SERVE 4.

SIMMERED FENNEL

Fennel's licorice flavor is somewhat muted here.

3 large fennel bulbs

2 tablespoons olive oil

2 cloves garlic, chopped fine

1 medium onion, chopped fine

½ cup vegetable broth, divided

½ cup dry white wine

½ cup cooked rice (optional)

2 tablespoons tomato sauce

salt and pepper

Trim fennel, cut into medium wedges, and set aside. Heat oil in a large saucepan. Add garlic and onion and sauté over medium heat until they begin to color, about 5 minutes. Add fennel, ¼ cup of the broth, wine, tomato sauce, rice (if used), and salt and pepper.

Cover and cook over low heat, stirring occasionally, until fennel is tender, about 20 minutes. Add broth as necessary to prevent sticking. The mixture should be moist but not swimming. Serve hot.

SERVES 4 TO 6.

FENNEL AU GRATIN

I use the water that steamed the fennel to cook rice for the same meal. It picks up just enough flavor to give the rice a certain something.

6 small fennel bulbs, halved, or larger equivalent, sliced thick

salt and pepper

1 cup chicken or vegetable broth

½ cup grated Parmesan cheese

3 tablespoons butter

Preheat oven to 400°F. Steam fennel for 12 to 15 minutes and drain. Arrange slices cut side up in a buttered 9-by-13-inch baking dish. Season to taste with salt and pepper and add chicken or vegetable broth. Sprinkle with cheese, dot with butter, and bake in upper third of oven for 30 minutes or until top is golden.

SERVES 6 TO 8.

KIMPIRA GOBO
STIR-FRIED BURDOCK

I got this recipe from my dear friend Debra Anderson-Frey, who got it from her grandmother in Hawaii. It goes wonderfully with fried tofu and other mild dishes. Peeling the slender, wiggly burdock roots is a bit frustrating, but everything else is easy. Dried shrimp are available in Asian markets. You are supposed to soak them first, but I like the texture when they are added to this dish dry.

1½ pounds gobo

2 tablespoons oil, divided

⅓ to ½ cup soy sauce

2 teaspoons sugar

¼ cup dried shrimp (optional)

½-inch piece of fresh chile pepper, chopped, or ¼ teaspoon dried red pepper flakes

Scrub gobo, peel, and slice into 2-inch matchsticks. Soak for 20 minutes in cold water. Mix 1 tablespoon of the oil, soy sauce, and sugar in a small bowl. Heat remaining tablespoon of oil in a medium skillet, add shrimp (if used), and sauté briefly over medium-high heat. Drain gobo, add to skillet, and cook 2 or 3 minutes. Add sauce and cook, stirring often, until most of the liquid is absorbed. Gobo should still be crisp. Add chile pepper or pepper flakes and serve.

SERVES 4.

ADOBO GREENS

Adobo is probably the best-known type of Filipino cooking. Usually it features chicken, pork, or a combination of the two, first marinated in a vinegar/soy sauce, then boiled, then fried. A similar treatment works well with greens, with lemon or lime juice substituted for vinegar. Try this with spinach, young chard, or mild mustard greens.

2 pounds fresh greens

3 cloves garlic, minced

1/3 cup oil

1 tablespoon lemon or lime juice

3 tablespoons soy sauce

1/2 teaspoon salt

pepper

Chop greens roughly. Cut small stems into bite-sized pieces; discard large ones. Heat oil in a large skillet, add garlic, and sauté until it turns golden. Add greens, sauté briefly, and then add lemon or lime juice, soy sauce, and salt. Cover and bring to a boil. Remove from heat, add pepper, and serve immediately.

SERVES 4.

GARBANZO BEANS WITH GREENS

Brief cooking gives this quick dish a fresh taste. It also can be served chilled.

3 tablespoons olive oil

1 tablepoon butter

1 garlic clove, minced or pressed

1 head escarole, cut across in 1/2-inch slices

1 teaspoon grated lemon peel (optional)

1/4 cup chopped parsley

salt and pepper

1 cup cooked garbanzo beans, drained

2 tablespoons lemon juice

Heat oil and butter in a large skillet until butter is melted. Add garlic and stir briefly over medium heat. Don't let it brown. Immediately add escarole to skillet and continue stirring over medium heat until it is wilted. Add lemon peel (if used) and parsley. Season with salt and pepper and mix in garbanzos. Stir gently over medium heat until beans are warmed through. Transfer to a serving bowl, sprinkle on lemon juice, and serve immediately.

SERVES 6.

Southern Mixed Greens

⬡ *Meals like these turned subsistence—foraged greens and scraps from the butchered hog—into something much better than just survival. Sliced oranges make a nice accompaniment, and they make me feel better about the vitamin C that has been cooked out of the greens. If you want to throw all cholesterol caution to the winds, cook the onions with ¼ pound of bacon and add the cooked bacon to the pot.*

3 pounds sturdy greens—collards, kale, beet greens, chard—coarsely chopped

2 ham hocks

1 quart water

1 teaspoon red pepper flakes

1 medium onion, chopped fine

2 tablespoons red wine vinegar

pepper

Trim excess fat from ham hocks and set it aside. Put ham hocks in a heavy saucepan or stove-top casserole. Cover with water, add red pepper flakes, and bring to a boil. Lower heat and simmer about 45 minutes.

Render some of the pork fat in a skillet. Add onions and cook slowly until they are soft and beginning to brown. Drain onions and add to ham-hock broth. Simmer another half hour or until meat begins to fall from bones.

Remove meat, trim off visible fat, and return meat to the pot. Stir in greens. Cover pot closely and cook about half an hour, stirring and lifting the greens occasionally.

Add vinegar and pepper to taste. The ham hocks should provide enough salt. Put meat and greens on a serving plate and serve pot liquor in separate small bowls. You'll want rice, biscuits, or cornbread to sop up the juice.

SERVES 4.

HORTOPITA

This Greek recipe is a country cousin of the richer spanakopita, which involves an egg and feta cheese custard along with spinach. I like to make it in February or March, when my overwintered greens are staging a comeback and the first wild greens are up. It should be made with filo dough, but in a pinch it's good with a light double pie crust.

1 pound mixed greens (I've used spinach, chard, romaine lettuce, rocket, nettles, sorrel, young beet greens, and turnip greens)

¼ cup olive oil

½ cup finely chopped leek or onion

6 sprigs mint, chopped

½ cup chopped parsley

4 tablespoons cooked rice

½ pound filo dough, or pastry for double-crust pie

¼ cup melted butter (if using filo dough)

Clean and stem greens. Steam leaves until limp, rinse in cold water, press out excess moisture, and chop fine. (If you have a great range of textures—say new sorrel and tough old chard—steam the vegetables separately.) Heat olive oil in heavy skillet. Add onion or leek and cook until soft. Add chopped greens, mint, and parsley and sauté for a few minutes. Stir in rice and cook until mixture is amalgamated. It should be fairly dry.

If using filo, pick up one sheet and place it gently in a shallow casserole or baking dish. Brush lightly with melted butter and repeat with half the filo. Skip the butter if you are using pie pastry. Spread filling over pastry and top with the rest of the buttered filo or the rest of the pastry. With a sharp knife, trim excess dough from around the edges. If using filo, bake 30 minutes at 350°F. If using pie pastry, start with 10 minutes at 425° and then reduce to 350° for another 20 minutes.

SERVES 4 TO 6.

SOY SAUCE VEGETABLES

This resembles the little pickled side dishes served at Japanese cafés. I like it best with turnips and daikon.

2 cups any firm vegetables—turnips, daikon, kohlrabi, carrots, beets, and so on

½ teaspoon salt

2 teaspoons sugar

mild soy sauce

Cut vegetables along the grain into julienne strips. Put them in a large jar with a lid. Add salt and sugar and shake well so that vegetables are coated. Let stand at room temperature for at least an hour or up to overnight.

Pour in enough soy sauce to cover vegetables. Press down to get rid of air pockets and let stand at room temperature for a day. Drain off soy sauce. (It can be reused for pickling or cooking.)

The vegetables will keep indefinitely in the refrigerator.

MAKES 2 CUPS.

JERUSALEM ARTICHOKES IN SOUR CREAM

I always use sour half-and-half in place of sour cream. Besides being marginally healthier, it is less likely to mask the flavor of the vegetables. You can make this dish in a flash with leftover baked Jerusalem artichokes, and it also is good made with scorzonera.

2 pounds Jerusalem artichokes (6 to 8 large), scrubbed and cooked

2 cups sour cream or sour half-and-half

3 tablespoons finely chopped onions

½ cup black olives, sliced

salt and pepper

paprika

chopped parsley

Dice cooked artichokes. Pour sour cream or sour half-and-half into skillet, add artichokes, and heat slowly over medium-low heat until liquid reaches a low boil. Simmer until artichokes are heated through. Add salt and pepper to taste and garnish with paprika and chopped parsley.

SERVES 8.

JERUSALEM ARTICHOKES WITH RICE

The original of this Turkish dish has a rather indigestible name, Zeytinyağli yer elmasiyra. *It is a sort of risotto, with the same moist texture as its Italian counterparts. Gentle-flavored and rather sweet, it is a good companion to a roast and a mixed green salad.*

4 tablespoons olive oil

1 small carrot, peeled and sliced thin

1 small onion, chopped

3 cups (about 1 pound) Jerusalem artichokes, scrubbed and cut into ½-inch cubes

juice of 1 lemon

salt and pepper

2 tablespoons long-grain rice

½ cup water

2 tablespoons chopped parsley

Heat oil in large, shallow saucepan or skillet. Add carrot and onion and sauté over medium heat for 5 minutes, until vegetables begin to soften. Add Jerusalem artichokes and cook another 2 minutes, stirring constantly. Add lemon juice, salt, pepper, rice, and water. Simmer, covered, until artichokes are tender and rice is soft, about 20 minutes. Add water as necessary, a little at a time, during cooking, but do not stir. The dish should be moist but not soupy. Serve at room temperature.

SERVES 4.

KALE SPROUTS

A kale-and-farewell suggestion for gardeners, from my friend Binda Colebrook:

When the flower buds start forming on your kale plants in the spring, pick stalks that are about half as long as asparagus. Cut off any tough parts and stick the bottoms of the stalks in a small, deep pan so the buds are at the top. Add a little water and boil, covered, for no more than 5 minutes. Serve with lemon and butter.

BAKED KOHLRABI AND FENNEL

A light sauce brings out the delicate flavors of kohlrabi and fennel.

1 fennel bulb

2 cups peeled kohlrabi, sliced about ½ inch thick

2 cups light soup stock (beef, chicken, or vegetable)

3 tablespoons butter, divided

2 tablespoons flour

salt and pepper

⅔ cup milk or half-and-half

¼ cup grated Parmesan cheese

½ teaspoon paprika

Preheat oven to 350°F. Strip stringy outer leaves of fennel. Slice to match kohlrabi. Bring stock to a boil, add vegetables, and cook until tender, about 7 to 10 minutes. Add enough stock to the milk or half-and-half to total 2 cups. Make a white sauce using 2 tablespoons of the butter, the flour, and the milk/stock mixture. Butter a casserole with remaining 1 tablespoon of butter and put in vegetables. Pour sauce over them, sprinkle with Parmesan cheese and paprika, and bake for about half an hour.

SERVES 4 TO 6.

LEEKS WITH LIME

This Indian dish is an interesting variation on leeks vinaigrette. Cooking time will vary with the size and firmness of your leeks. They should end up tender but not mucilaginous.

2 cloves garlic

6 medium leeks, washed and trimmed

1 cup water

½ teaspoon saffron (optional)

1 teaspoon salt

2-inch stick cinnamon

2 bay leaves

2 teaspoons olive oil

½ teaspoon black pepper

½ teaspoon chili powder

½ teaspoon mace

juice of 6 limes or 3 large lemons

Peel and crush garlic and rub cloves over leeks. Reserve garlic for marinade. Simmer leeks, water, saffron (if used), salt, cinnamon, and bay leaves for 15 minutes. Remove leeks from pan and return liquid to heat. Boil gently until reduced by half. Remove from heat and cool. Discard cinnamon stick and bay leaves. Beat in olive oil, pepper, chili powder, and mace. Add reserved garlic and lime or lemon juice, pour over leeks, and marinate at least 2 hours.

SERVES 4.

STIR-FRIED LEEKS AND ROMAINE

Romaine makes a fine stir-fry green. Don't turn your back on it, though—it cooks almost instantly. Rice vinegar is standard for this sauce, but I like it with raspberry vinegar.

¼ cup water

2 tablespoons soy sauce

2 tablespoons rice vinegar or raspberry vinegar

3 tablespoons vegetable oil

4 medium leeks, white and light green, cut in half and sliced thin

1 medium head romaine, shredded

1 teaspoon red pepper flakes

Combine water, soy sauce, and vinegar in a small bowl and set aside. Heat oil in wok or large skillet. Add leeks, tossing to coat evenly. Stir over high heat for 30 seconds. Add romaine and toss to combine.

Pour on soy mixture and reduce heat. Sprinkle with red pepper flakes. Continue stirring over medium heat until all the liquid is evaporated. Serve at once.

SERVES 4.

BASQUE LEEKS

These can go next to the salmon in the last outdoor grilling of the season or under the broiler indoors. Leeks can also be trimmed, washed, steamed lightly, and then briefly broiled without the foil wrapping. Sprinkle with salt and pepper and brush with olive oil as they cook.

12 medium leeks

1 tablespoon olive oil or unsalted butter

salt and pepper

Position broiler rack 4 inches from heat source and preheat. Trim all but 1 inch of green from leeks. Remove any tough outer leaves. Beginning about 1 inch from base, split leeks upward, using a sharp, thin knife.

Wash leeks thoroughly, drain, and pat dry. Arrange on a large sheet of heavy aluminum foil. Rub each leek with olive oil or dot with butter. Sprinkle with salt and pepper to taste. Enclose completely in foil, wrapping tightly. Transfer to broiler pan or baking sheet. Broil 5 minutes on each side. Serve immediately.

SERVES 6.

GREEN PASTA WITH LEEKS AND OLIVES

Rich and slightly sweet, this goes well with broiled fish or fettuccine.

½ pound dried spinach spaghetti or fettuccine

4 tablespoons butter, divided

3 medium leeks, including tops, sliced thin

1 cup whipping cream

1 small can chopped black olives

salt and pepper

nutmeg

Melt 3 tablespoons of the butter in a medium saucepan over medium heat. Add leeks and cook, stirring occasionally, until softened but not browned, about 10 minutes. Blend in cream and cook, uncovered, over medium heat, stirring frequently, until sauce thickens, about another 10 minutes. Add salt, pepper, olives, and nutmeg, and heat through. Remove from heat and keep warm while pasta cooks.

Cook pasta al dente, drain, and transfer to heated serving platter. Add sauce and remaining butter and toss lightly.

SERVES 6.

SAFFRON LEEKS AND POTATOES

This Spanish combination is addictive. My only complaint is that I never have leftovers. It makes a good main dish as long as you have a bit more protein elsewhere in the meal.

3 tablespoons olive oil

3 garlic cloves, sliced

3 large leeks, trimmed, with some green, cut into 3-inch strips

½ cup tomato sauce

pinch of saffron, crumbled and soaked in a little water

salt and pepper

1 pound potatoes (3 medium), peeled and sliced into ½-inch rounds

2 tablespoons chopped parsley

Heat oil in a large skillet or shallow saucepan, add garlic, and sauté for 2 minutes. Add leeks, tomato sauce, saffron and water, salt, pepper, and enough water to barely cover vegetables. Simmer, covered, 10 minutes. Add potatoes and parsley. Mix well, cover, and simmer until the potatoes are tender and water is absorbed, about 15 minutes. Serve hot.

SERVES 4.

LEEKS IN POOR MAN'S SAUCE

Poor Man's Sauce is a very old recipe, a strongly flavored vinaigrette. It's good on a variety of cold cooked vegetables, including carrots, broccoli, and Jerusalem artichokes.

12 medium leeks, with 2 inches of green

1 cup Poor Man's Sauce (see recipe below)

2 hard-boiled eggs, sieved or chopped fine

½ teaspoon dried tarragon

½ teaspoon dried basil

2 tablespoons chopped parsley

Trim leeks and cut in half lengthwise. Steam until tender, remove from heat, and cool. Mix Poor Man's Sauce with eggs, tarragon, basil, and parsley and pour over leeks. Chill at least 1 hour.

Poor Man's Sauce

4 green onions or small leeks, minced

2 tablespoons chopped parsley

2 shallots, minced, or 1 tablespoon finely chopped onion

3 tablespoons red wine vinegar

½ cup olive oil

salt and pepper

Put all ingredients in a jar with a tight lid. Shake well.

SERVES 4.

SAUTÉED LETTUCE WITH ROSEMARY

In December, when I am harvesting my precious lettuce plants leaf by leaf, the last thing I want to do is cook them. Come March, however, I sometimes have a surplus of overwintered plants, and it's a shame to let them bolt. Served with a rosemary-flavored cream sauce, weatherbeaten lettuce can rise to elegance. Rosemary is surprisingly hardy. A pot I left out during a 10-degree cold snap and ice storm looked dead in April but had sent out new sprouts by June. If you actually want it to grow in winter, however, you should bring it inside to a sunny windowsill. Unlike a lot of plants, it doesn't mind dry winter houses.

1/4 pound (1 1/2 cups) sliced mushrooms

6 tablespoons butter, divided

2 tablespoons flour

2/3 cup chicken broth

2/3 cup light cream

salt and pepper

1/4 teaspoon nutmeg

1 teaspoon fresh rosemary

1 tablespoon chopped parsley

2 tablespoons Cognac (optional)

2 large or 3 small heads Boston lettuce

2 tablespoons chopped chives

Sauté mushrooms briefly in 4 tablespoons of the butter. Sprinkle with flour. Slowly stir in broth and cream and bring to a boil, stirring. Season with salt and pepper, nutmeg, rosemary, parsley, and Cognac (if used). Hold over hot water.

Shred lettuce into very wide ribbons and sauté briefly in remaining butter just until wilted. Toss lettuce with sauce, sprinkle with chives, and serve immediately.

SERVES 4.

WHOLE GRAIN PASTA WITH ONION SAUCE

I've never been happy with whole wheat pastas, much as I approve of the idea. Something about their gritty texture just doesn't seem right. (I do like the sesame-rice spirals sold in health food stores.) However, their variety is increasing, their quality is improving, and the right sauce can make a big difference. Unlike more refined pasta dishes, where the sauce provides texture as well as flavor, what you want with whole wheat is something with plenty of taste but a very smooth feel. This slow-cooked onion mixture is just right. Mix with a few anchovies and you've got an excellent pizza topping.

5 tablespoons olive oil, divided

2 pounds onions, sliced thin

1/2 teaspoon red pepper flakes, or more to taste

salt and pepper

2 tablespoons chopped parsley

1/2 cup Parmesan cheese

1 pound whole grain pasta

Heat 3 tablespoons of the olive oil in a large skillet, add onions and red pepper flakes, cover, and cook over low heat for 15 minutes, stirring occasionally. Remove cover, raise heat to medium, and cook until onions brown, about 10 minutes more. Add salt, pepper, parsley, remaining 2 tablespoons of olive oil, and Parmesan cheese. Set aside.

Meanwhile, bring 4 quarts salted water to a boil, add pasta, and cook, uncovered, until pasta is al dente. Drain pasta, mix with sauce, and serve immediately. Pass more Parmesan.

SERVES 6.

CIDER-GLAZED PARSNIPS

The quality of the cider makes a difference here. If you can, splurge on unfiltered, unreconstituted, preferably unpasteurized cider.

4 medium parsnips

2 tablespoons butter

¼ cup fresh sweet cider

salt and pepper

¼ teaspoon freshly grated nutmeg

Wash and peel parsnips and cook in lightly salted boiling water for about 10 minutes. Drain and slice, discarding any woody core.

Melt butter in frying pan and add cider. Bring to boil, add parsnips, and cook uncovered at medium heat until liquid has evaporated and parsnips are beginning to color. Sprinkle with nutmeg.

SERVES 6.

BAKED PARSNIPS

Simple and unadorned, this dish shows the superiority of garden parsnips. Try it after a frost. The same treatment is good with Jerusalem artichokes. Leave small ones whole; halve or quarter larger ones.

4 medium parsnips, trimmed and scrubbed

4 tablespoons butter

salt and pepper

Preheat oven to 400°F. Quarter parsnips and cut them into pieces about 4 inches long. Melt butter in an oven-proof baking dish. Add parsnips, turn to coat, and bake uncovered for 30 to 45 minutes until lightly browned and tender. Turn once or twice during cooking so they color evenly. Season with salt and pepper and serve.

This is also great with roast meat or poultry. When the roast comes out, just put the parsnips in the roasting pan, roll them in the fat and juices, and bake for about 20 minutes. Serve with the sliced meat.

SERVES 6.

ENGLISH PARSNIP PIE

Parsnip pie is traditionally made with a lattice crust and decorated with primroses, a celebration of early spring. It is a side dish rather than a dessert and goes well with roast meat or poultry.

2 pounds parsnips

1 teaspoon salt

2 tablespoons honey

pinch of ginger

¼ teaspoon cinnamon

1 tablespoon fresh orange juice

2 teaspoons grated fresh orange rind (optional)

2 eggs, slightly beaten

pastry for single-crust 9-inch pie, partially baked, with extra for lattice if you wish

Preheat oven to 375°F. Steam parsnips until tender, about 20 minutes. Drain, cool enough to handle, and chop fine. Combine in a medium bowl with salt, honey, ginger, cinnamon, orange juice, orange rind (if used), and eggs. Mix well. Pour into pastry shell and top with lattice if desired. Bake 30 minutes.

SERVES 8.

POTATO WATERCRESS PURÉE

The bright, blanched watercress turns these mashed potatoes a real St. Patrick's Day green. The flavor is fresh rather than peppery.

2 bunches watercress, leaves only

⅔ cup whipping cream

2 pounds potatoes

salt and pepper

butter

1 tablespoon minced parsley

Put all but 1 tablespoon of watercress leaves in a colander. Immerse colander for 30 seconds in a large saucepan of boiling water. Transfer leaves to blender, add cream, and purée until smooth. Peel potatoes and boil until tender. Drain and mash, mixing in salt, pepper, and butter to taste. Add watercress cream and stir. Garnish with parsley and reserved water-cress leaves.

SERVES 4 TO 6.

ROAST POTATOES WITH ROSEMARY

Really fresh, new potatoes are sweet enough to eat raw. You won't get that kind of flavor from winter storage potatoes, which have long since converted their sugar into starch, but they still can taste wonderful without a lot of fuss or sour cream. This dish needs fresh herbs. Oregano (which grows all winter in my garden) can be used instead of rosemary. The best potatoes for roasting are thin-skinned varieties like White Rose and Yellow Finn. Big, floury baking potatoes won't work as well.

2 pounds potatoes, the smaller and younger the better, scrubbed and cut into 1-inch cubes

leaves from 4 large sprigs fresh rosemary

4 large cloves garlic, peeled and crushed

1/2 cup olive oil

salt and pepper

1 tablespoon chopped parsley

Preheat oven to 425°F. Place potatoes, rosemary, and garlic in a roasting pan, pour olive oil over, and add salt and pepper to taste. Bake, stirring occasionally, until potatoes are browned and crisp on the outside, tender on the inside, about 30 to 40 minutes. Sprinkle with parsley and serve.

SERVES 6.

COLCANNON

An old Irish dish, with lots of variations. Similar recipes turn up in Wales, Scotland, England, and Holland, and probably other nations too. It shows up on a lot of Irish tables at Halloween and on Irish-American tables on St. Patrick's Day, along with the corned beef and soda bread. Precise measurements seem to violate the spirit of this kind of cooking, so herewith a recipe from a 19th-century American cookbook by Miss Eliza Leslie, quoted in James Beard's American Cookery. *I would steam the cabbage instead of boiling it.*

Boil separately some potatoes and cabbage. When done, drain and squeeze the cabbage, and chop, or mince it very small. Mash the potatoes, and mix them gradually but thoroughly with the chopped cabbage, adding butter, pepper and salt. There should be twice as much potato as cabbage.

STAMPOT

Stampot is to Dutch cooks what colcannon is to the Irish.

Add an equal portion of hot, mashed potatoes to hot, cooked kale, cabbage, sauerkraut, or chopped beets. Mash together, add some butter and a little milk, and salt and pepper to taste. This has made many a meal, perhaps with a little bacon or sausage on the side.

KOFTESI

These Turkish potato pancakes are quick (if you have some leftover cooked potatoes), easy, and attractive, with cheerful flecks of red and green. They make a good lunch along with a bowl of soup or a salad.

2 pounds potatoes (about 6 medium), cooked and mashed

2 tablespoons melted butter

2 tablespoons chopped parsley

6 scallions or 3 slender leeks, white part only, chopped

½ cup canned plum tomatoes, drained, seeded, and chopped

1 cup fine dry bread crumbs

½ cup cottage cheese

1 egg, lightly beaten

salt and pepper

about ½ cup sifted flour

olive oil

Preheat oven to 400°F. Coat a baking sheet with olive oil. Put mashed potatoes in a medium bowl and add, in order, butter, parsley, scallions, tomatoes, bread crumbs, cottage cheese, and egg, stirring after each addition. When mixture is well blended, add salt and pepper and work in just enough flour to make a stiff dough.

Press spoonfuls of dough into patties on a floured board, or pat into shape with your floured hands. Put patties on baking sheet, brush tops with olive oil, and bake until golden, about 15 minutes.

MAKES 2 DOZEN 3-INCH
PATTIES.

PUMPKIN-CHEESE PANCAKES

These little golden pancakes are a hit at our house with no condiments necessary. They could be dressed up with a spoonful of sour cream or yogurt. I use a blender to mix the ingredients. If you are doing it by hand, be sure to cook the pumpkin until it is really soft.

2 tablespoons butter or vegetable oil

2 medium leeks or large scallions, sliced into rounds

2 cups grated peeled pumpkin or other winter squash

salt and pepper

$1/4$ teaspoon nutmeg

2 eggs

6 tablespoons milk

6 tablespoons flour

$1/4$ cup grated Jarlsberg or Parmesan cheese

Melt butter or oil in a heavy, medium-sized skillet over medium-low heat. Add leeks and stir 1 minute. Add pumpkin, salt, pepper, and nutmeg. Cook until pumpkin is tender, stirring frequently, about 5 minutes. Remove from heat and let cool while you start the batter.

Beat together eggs, milk, flour, and cheese. Add pumpkin mixture and blend. Butter a large, heavy skillet and heat to medium–high. Lower heat to medium and make small pancakes, using about 2 tablespoons of batter for each. Cook about 45 seconds per side. Serve on a warmed plate, sprinkled with a little more nutmeg.

SERVES 4 AS A SIDE DISH
OR 2 AS A MAIN DISH.

BROILED RADICCHIO

This couldn't be easier, and it makes an excellent foil for the mild risottos and polentas of the Veneto region of Italy, where it originates. It's also a good use for slightly ragged-looking plants.

¹/₂ cup olive oil

2 cloves garlic, sliced

2 tablespoons fresh lemon juice

salt and pepper

2 medium heads radicchio

Preheat broiler to 450°F. Heat olive oil in a small skillet, add garlic, and cook over low heat until garlic begins to turn color. Remove from heat and strain out garlic. Add lemon juice, salt, and pepper.

Cut radicchio in half lengthwise and brush surface with olive oil mixture. Place cut side down on a hot broiling pan. Cook 3 to 5 minutes, turning once, until radicchio is dull brown and edges are slightly crisped. Transfer to plates and pour remaining oil over the top.

SERVES 4.

LE GOURMAND SALSIFY

Bruce Naftaly and Robin Saunders serve this as an appetizer at Le Gourmand in Seattle.

1 pound salsify or scorzonera

1 cup heavy cream

nutmeg

¹/₈ teaspoon white pepper

1 tablespoon chopped chervil, Italian parsley, or sweet cicely

salt

Peel salsify or scorzonera and cut into pieces the size of your little finger. Put cut pieces in acidulated water as you go. Drain, then steam until barely tender, about 5 minutes.

Combine cream, nutmeg, pepper, and herbs in a heavy, nonaluminum saucepan or sauté pan. Bring to a boil, lower heat, and cook gently until cream is reduced almost to the consistency of sauce. Add salsify or scorzonera and continue cooking until liquid makes a sauce. Add salt to taste.

SERVES 3 OR 4.

SCORZONERA WITH SOUR CREAM

The full flavor of scorzonera (or salsify, its taste twin) can hold its own with this rich sauce.

2 pounds scorzonera (6 to 8 roots), peeled

1 medium onion, minced

2 tablespoons butter

1 tablespoon flour

1 cup sour cream or sour half-and-half

salt and pepper

2 tablespoons grated Swiss cheese

2 tablespoons bread crumbs

Preheat oven to 400°F. Steam scorzonera until tender, about 8 minutes. Remove from heat and dice when cool enough to handle. Mix together scorzonera and onion and spoon into greased casserole. Melt butter in small saucepan. Stir in flour and simmer 1 minute. Add sour cream or sour half-and-half and salt and pepper to taste. Heat gently; don't let it boil. Spoon mixture over vegetables and toss lightly to blend. Sprinkle with grated Swiss cheese and crumbs. Bake 15 to 20 minutes.

SERVES 4 TO 6.

PURÉED SORREL

Sorrel cooks so quickly that this useful combination can be ready in minutes. It makes a good sauce or omelet filling. Don't use an aluminum or cast-iron pan.

2 pounds of sorrel, washed and stemmed

¼ cup heavy cream

salt and pepper

nutmeg

Blanch sorrel for 2 to 3 minutes. Drain, press out excess water, and purée. Pour sorrel into a deep saucepan, whisk in cream, and heat gently just until mixture thickens. Season to taste with salt, pepper, and nutmeg.

MAKES 2½ CUPS.

SHIKUMCHEE
(KOREAN SPINACH AND GARLIC)

During the Seattle World's Fair of 1962, a family of musicians opened what I think was the first Korean restaurant in Seattle. I had this spinach there as a child, served with elegant metal chopsticks, and I never forgot it. Once they had paid Juilliard tuition for their children, the parents closed the business and retired. Steamed carrot matchsticks can be treated the same way, and they look nice on a plate with the spinach.

2 teaspoons sugar

3 tablespoons soy sauce

2 tablespoons toasted sesame seeds

¼ cup minced scallions or small leeks

1 tablespoon toasted sesame seed oil

1 tablespoon minced garlic

2 pounds fresh spinach leaves

Combine all ingredients except spinach in a mixing bowl and blend well. Just before serving, steam spinach leaves over boiling water. Chop coarsely. Arrange on warm serving platter. Pour sauce over and serve immediately.

DRY SPINACH CURRY

This curry is served in small portions as a condiment in an Indian meal.

¼ cup ghee (see page 218) or mild oil

1 medium onion, chopped fine

2 cloves garlic, chopped fine

2 small green chiles, seeds and ribs removed, cut into ¼-inch pieces

1 pound spinach, washed, drained, and coarsely chopped

salt and black pepper

Heat ghee or oil in heavy saucepan. Add onion and garlic and sauté until they begin to turn color, but do not let them brown. Add chiles and continue cooking a minute. Add spinach, turning constantly. Add a sprinkle of water if necessary. Add salt and pepper and cook until done.

SERVES 3 OR 4.

SPINACH WITH RAISINS AND PINE NUTS

Pine nuts are a 25-mile drive away from my house. Sunflower seeds aren't the same, but they make an acceptable variation. Increase the steaming time if you substitute young chard leaves for the spinach. A Catalonian version of this Mediterranean dish adds 2 anchovy fillets along with the garlic. Cook them gently until they dissolve.

2 pounds spinach or chard

¼ cup raisins

¼ cup pine nuts

¼ cup olive oil

2 garlic cloves, peeled and crushed

salt and pepper

Steam spinach or chard (about 5 minutes for spinach or 10 minutes for chard) and chop coarsely. Plump raisins in warm water and drain. Toss raisins and pine nuts with spinach or chard and set aside.

Heat oil in a large skillet and sauté garlic gently until cooked but not brown. Add spinach or chard mixture, toss well, cover, and simmer for 5 minutes. Uncover and raise heat if necessary to evaporate excess moisture. Season to taste with salt and pepper and serve at once.

SERVES 4.

SPINACH SESAME PURÉE

This has the flavor of Japanese spinach salad, with a much different texture.

2 pounds spinach, washed and trimmed

2 tablespoons butter

2 tablespoons toasted sesame seeds

1 tablespoon chopped chives

Steam spinach until soft, drain thoroughly, chop, and purée. Melt butter in small saucepan over low heat. Stir in spinach and sesame seeds and cook until heated through. Remove from heat and blend in chives.

SERVES 3 OR 4.

MOROCCAN SQUASH PURÉE

◈ *This is a new approach to squash for most people, and I think it's great. The spicy taste is unusual, but it's neither red-hot nor intimidating.*

2 tablespoons olive oil

1½ pounds winter squash, peeled, seeded, and cut into 1-inch cubes

3 cloves garlic, chopped

½ cup water

1 tablespoon chopped parsley

1 tablespoon chopped cilantro

pinch of saffron (optional), crumbled in ¼ cup warm water

1 teaspoon ground ginger

¼ cup lemon juice

1 tablespoon sugar

¼ teaspoon cayenne

salt and pepper

1 tablespoon ground cumin

Heat olive oil in a wide saucepan or skillet. Add squash, garlic, and water. Cover and cook, stirring frequently, for 15 to 20 minutes or until squash is tender. Combine rest of ingredients except cumin. Pour over squash and simmer, covered, another 10 minutes. Add a little water if necessary to prevent sticking. The squash will start to disintegrate.

Sprinkle with cumin and serve warm.

SERVES 4.

SWEET POTATOES AND APPLES
WITH MAPLE GLAZE

The idea is to set off the sweet potatoes with a bit of tartness and then bring the dish together with the flavor of maple syrup. It's a good plan, easily executed.

3 pounds baked sweet potatoes or yams

3 cooking apples

¼ cup fresh lemon juce

4 tablespoons butter

¼ cup firmly packed brown sugar

½ cup maple syrup

½ teaspoon cinnamon

2 tablespoons dark rum (optional)

Preheat oven to 400°F. Put rack at highest position. Use some of the butter to prepare a large baking pan or gratin dish. Let sweet potatoes cool slightly, cut off ends, pull off peel with dull knife, and cut on the diagonal into ¼-inch slices.

Peel and core apples and cut lengthwise into ½-inch slices. Put into a bowl and toss with lemon juice. Place in baking pan, overlapping slices slightly and making a nice pattern of sweet potato and apple.

Combine butter, sugar, maple syrup, cinnamon, and rum (if used) in a small saucepan and stir over medium heat until sugar dissolves. Pour mixture slowly over apples and sweet potatoes so that top is uniformly moistened. Bake in upper third of oven, basting frequently, for 25 minutes or until apples are tender and sweet potatoes have a nice glaze. Broil for 20 seconds if edges aren't browned.

SERVES 6 TO 8.

OVEN-ROASTED SWEET POTATOES

The dark sauce makes this dish look a little strange, but it tastes great.

6 tablespoons butter

1 clove garlic, sliced

two 8-ounce yams *or* 2 medium sweet potatoes

4 tablespoons soy sauce

2 tablespoons red wine vinegar

2 tablespoons sugar

dash of hot pepper sauce

Melt butter in a small saucepan. Add garlic and remove from heat. Let stand 15 minutes. Preheat oven to 375°F. Peel yams and cut lengthwise into wedges. Remove garlic from butter and discard. Pour butter into baking dish. Add yams, turning to coat evenly with butter. Bake 30 minutes.

Meanwhile, combine soy sauce, wine vinegar, sugar, and hot pepper sauce in a small bowl. Stir until sugar is dissolved. Brush over yams and bake another 15 to 20 minutes until tender.

SERVES 4.

SWISS CHARD AND OLIVES

The emphatic flavors of Provençal and North African cuisines go well with tough winter chard. The tians of Provence combine chard with anchovies or even salt cod. Moroccan dishes, such as this one, use pungent olives and preserved lemons. Widely used in North Africa, preserved lemons were at one time a craze in the U.S. (Does anyone remember when Amy's love of pickled lemons got her into trouble in Little Women?*) They are quick to prepare, but they should cure for a month before using. This recipe is good—though not the same—without them. Do not substitute fresh lemon.*

2 pounds chard (stems removed), roughly chopped, or 1 pound each chard and spinach

4 tablespoons olive oil

2 cloves garlic, chopped

1 tablespoon sweet paprika

2 teaspoons turmeric

¼ teaspoon pepper

6 large green or black Greek or Italian olives, pitted, rinsed, and chopped

rind of 1 preserved lemon (optional), rinsed and cut into thin wedges

Bring ½ cup water to a boil in a saucepan, add chard, reduce heat, and simmer, covered, until tender, about 10 minutes. Drain. If you are using both chard and spinach, cook the spinach separately for about 5 minutes in the water that remains on the leaves after washing. Drain well.

Heat oil in a heavy saucepan or skillet. Add garlic and sauté over medium heat for 1 minute. Add paprika, turmeric, and pepper and mix well. Add greens and olives and toss to blend thoroughly. Continue cooking, stirring constantly, for 3 or 4 minutes. Add preserved lemon (if used), cook another 2 minutes, and serve hot.

Preserved lemons

5 or 6 small, thin-skinned lemons or limes

⅓ cup salt

juice of 2 lemons

Cut lemons or limes almost through from the blossom end into quarters, leaving them in one piece at the stem end. Sprinkle each with 1 teaspoon of salt and fit it together again. Place fruit in a sterilized 1-quart wide-mouth glass jar, squeezing snugly to fit. Add remaining salt, lemon juice, and enough warm water to cover. Close jar and shake to dissolve the salt. Let stand for a month in a dark place. Don't worry if the lemons get a bit scummy; the scum is harmless and it rinses off. These will keep for up to a year. You can use just the skin, as is traditional, or the whole lemon.

SERVES 4.

SWISS CHARD PARMIGIANA

Most chard recipes call for the leaves only, but some cuisines value the wide stems enough to raise special broad-stemmed varieties. Blanching removes the somewhat metallic flavor of older specimens.

12 to 16 large chard stalks (from about 2 pounds of fresh chard), cut into 4-inch lengths and blanched

salt and pepper

$\frac{1}{2}$ to $\frac{2}{3}$ cup grated Parmesan cheese

6 tablespoons melted butter

Preheat oven to 400° F. Butter a 9-by-12-inch baking dish and make a single layer of drained chard stems. Season with salt and pepper and sprinkle with $\frac{1}{3}$ of the cheese and a drizzle of butter. Make two more layers in this manner, saving enough cheese and butter for a good coating on top. Bake 20 minutes or until top is golden. Let stand 10 minutes or so before serving.

SERVES 4.

SWISS CHARD STALKS BEURRE NOIR

If you have fresh sage, sauté it until it starts to get crisp. The salt in the butter may be enough for the dish. If not, salt to taste.

12 to 16 large chard stalks, cut into 4-inch lengths

3 tablespoons butter

$\frac{1}{2}$ teaspoon finely chopped fresh sage, or $\frac{1}{4}$ teaspoon dried basil

pepper

$\frac{1}{2}$ teaspoon lemon juice

Steam chard stalks until barely tender. Heat butter in a medium skillet, stirring constantly until it starts to brown. Add sage or basil, pepper, and lemon juice and pour over chard stalks.

SERVES 4.

TURNIPS IN MAPLE MUSTARD SAUCE

A sweet and spicy sauce picks up the blander sweetness of cooked turnips (or parsnips) and transports it to a better world.

2 pounds white turnips or parsnips

4 tablespoons butter

1 tablespoon English dry mustard

1 tablespoon dark brown sugar

2 tablespoons maple syrup

salt and pepper

Preheat oven to 350°F. Peel and slice turnips or parsnips and blanch in boiling water for 3 to 5 minutes. You don't want them to get mushy. Drain vegetables and set aside to cool. Melt butter in a covered casserole or baking dish. Stir in dry mustard, brown sugar, maple syrup, salt, and pepper. Work each vegetable slice into sauce and arrange slices in a nice pattern. Bake, covered, for 30 minutes.

SERVES 4 TO 6.

TURNIPS WITH ANCHOVIES

This Italian dish is best with small young turnips, but it works fine with bigger ones provided their flavor is good. Old, hot, corky turnips are no good for this (or anything else). The same recipe, minus the rosemary, can be used for turnip greens.

3 tablespoons olive oil

4 garlic cloves, sliced thin

3 anchovy fillets, drained and cut into small pieces

2 tablespoons fresh rosemary or 1 tablespoon dried

2 pounds turnips, peeled and sliced thin

salt and pepper to taste

1 tablespoon minced parsley

Heat oil in saucepan or medium skillet. Add garlic, anchovies, and rosemary and sauté over medium-low heat for 1 minute. Don't let the garlic brown.

Add turnips, season with salt and pepper, and sauté, stirring frequently, until tender, about 8 to 10 minutes. Sprinkle with parsley and serve hot.

SERVES 6.

SAUCES

Skordalia

This Greek dip is good news for garlic lovers. It is traditionally served with fried foods. We also like it with antipasto vegetables or with boiled beets. Once you have the basic idea, there are many traditional variations. Fish stock can be added to make a pourable sauce. Walnuts can be substituted for the potato, and vinegar for the lemon juice.

5 slices dense white bread, crusts removed

at least 3 large cloves garlic, crushed

1 medium potato, peeled, boiled, and drained

¼ teaspoon salt

⅓ cup olive oil

3 tablespoons lemon juice

Wet bread with cold water, squeeze out moisture, and crumble into a blender. Add garlic and process. Add boiled potato and salt and process again. Pour in oil in a slow, steady stream and then add lemon juice. Taste and add more salt or lemon juice if needed. The mixture should be stiff and shiny. It will keep 10 days in the refrigerator and tastes best after a day or two.

MAKES 2 CUPS.

WILD SORREL AND NETTLE SAUCE

The chefs at Sooke Harbour House serve this sauce with sautéed abalone. Try it also with scallops, shrimp, or fish.

3 tablespoons minced shallots

3 tablespoons clarified unsalted butter

1 large clove garlic, minced

24 wild sorrel leaves, or 15 leaves of cultivated sorrel

24 young nettle leaves

2 cups fish stock

¼ cup dry white wine

1 cup heavy cream

3 tablespoons cold unsalted butter, in small pieces

edible flowers for garnish (optional)—freesias, calendula, mustard flowers, chickweed flowers

Melt butter in a saucepan and sauté shallots and garlic until soft. Add sorrel and nettles and sauté gently for about a minute. Add fish stock and wine and bring to a boil. Boil gently until liquid is reduced by half. Purée mixture in blender and then pass through a fine sieve. Pour back into pot and add cream. Simmer 5 minutes or until thickened. Remove from heat and whisk in cold butter.

Spoon sauce onto plates and arrange seafood on top. Garnish with edible flowers, if available.

MAKES 2 CUPS.

SEAFOOD SAUCE

I don't know what seafood is most popular in Angola, where this sauce is from, but I have served it with broiled salmon to great acclaim.

2 cloves garlic, crushed

½ cup chopped green onions or chives

4 tablespoons chopped parsley

1 teaspoon ground cumin

¼ teaspoon salt

4 tablespoons vinegar

4 tablespoons water

Combine all ingredients and process briefly in blender or food processor, or grind herbs and spices with a mortar and pestle and then stir in vinegar and water. Chill before serving.

MAKES 1 CUP.

GHEE

Melt at least one stick of unsalted butter in a shallow pot over very low heat. It must not brown. Skim froth that rises to top, repeating the process until you have a clear yellowish liquid. Cool a few minutes, pour off the clear liquid, and strain though muslin to catch the last particles. Refrigerate in a covered jar. The ghee will solidify. Warm gently to liquefy before using in cooking. It will keep indefinitely.

NITER KIBBEH
CLARIFIED BUTTER WITH SPICES

Like Indian ghee, this Ethiopian preparation solves the problem of storing butter without refrigeration. You probably don't have to worry about that, but if you want to turn the simplest steamed vegetables or boiled potatoes into something special, look no further.

1 pound unsalted butter

4 tablespoons chopped onion

1½ tablespoons chopped garlic

2 teaspoons grated fresh ginger

½ teaspoon turmeric

2 whole cardamom seeds, crushed, or ½ teaspoon ground cardamom

1-inch stick of cinnamon

2 or 3 whole cloves

⅛ teaspoon ground nutmeg

Slowly melt butter in a saucepan and then bring it to a boil. When butter is covered with foam, add all remaining ingredients, lower heat, and simmer, uncovered, over very low heat until the surface is transparent and the milk solids are on the bottom. This can take up to an hour. Pour off the clear liquid (leaving as much residue as possible in the pan) and strain through a double layer of damp cheesecloth. Strain twice more if you expect to keep the *niter kibbeh* for more than a few weeks. After three strainings it should keep for two to three months, even at room temperature.

MAKES ABOUT 2 CUPS.

MINT CHUTNEY

A wonderful East African sauce for grilled fish and chicken or seafood curries. It will keep several weeks refrigerated in a tightly closed jar.

½ cup fresh mint leaves

½ cup coriander leaves

handful of roasted peanuts or cashews

3 or 4 cloves garlic

juice of 2 limes

2 teaspoons coriander seeds, crushed

1 tablespoon sugar

1 mildly hot pepper

pinch of cayenne

Combine all ingredients in blender and whirl until well mixed. Pour into a clean jar and cover tightly.

MAKES ABOUT 1 CUP.

CRANBERRY HORSERADISH RELISH

Two cups is a lot of relish, but this tangy combination improves with age. It is a Russian recipe, meant for boiled beef or pot roast. It's also sensational on a broiled Swiss cheese sandwich. Use fresh horseradish if you possibly can.

½ pound cranberries

½ cup light brown sugar

¼ cup grated fresh or bottled horseradish

2 tablespoons fresh lemon juice

Chop cranberries medium fine. (The job will be easier if you freeze them first.) Stir in remaining ingredients and mix well. Refrigerate for at least 2 days before serving.

MAKES 2 CUPS.

PICKLED JERUSALEM ARTICHOKES

A simple condiment, good in salads, from Bruce Naftaly at Le Gourmand in Seattle. Naftaly uses an aged sherry vinegar. You might want to make a few test batches before settling on the right flavor for your kitchen.

2 cups sliced Jerusalem artichokes

your favorite vinegar

Peel Jerusalem artichokes and slice thin. Keep peeled artichokes in acidulated water and return slices to acidulated water. When finished, drain and place slices in a glass jar. Pour vinegar over to cover. Refrigerate, covered, for at least 5 days before using. The pickles will keep indefinitely.

MAKES 2 CUPS.

BROCCOLI SAUCE

This is a good use for leftover broccoli or for those last side shoots in the garden that are too skinny to serve on their own. Serve over brown rice or a substantial pasta. Follow with a custard or a clafouti for a simple, high-protein vegetarian meal.

2 cups cooked broccoli

1/3 cup olive oil

1/3 cup red wine vinegar or balsamic vinegar

1/2 teaspoon basil

1/4 teaspoon cumin

salt and pepper

1 tablespoon tomato paste

Combine all ingredients and purée. Reheat gently in small saucepan if broccoli is cold.

SERVES 4.

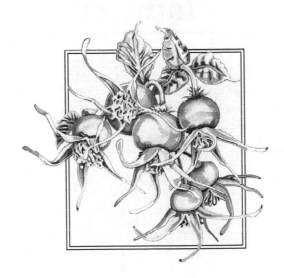

DESSERTS AND
BAKED GOODS

CELERIAC BREAD

I brought this savory bread to a potluck and watched people go back for slice after slice as they tried to figure out the secret ingredients. The texture is light and flaky, rather like that of a biscuit.

3 cups flour

¼ teaspoon baking powder

1 teaspoon baking soda

1 teaspoon salt

3 eggs

⅔ cup oil

2 cups grated celeriac

½ cup minced onion

1 tablespoon parsley

¼ teaspoon dried marjoram

⅛ teaspoon pepper

butter

1 tablespoon flour

Preheat oven to 350°F. Sift together flour, baking powder, baking soda, and salt. In large bowl, beat eggs and then add oil, celeriac, onion, parsley, marjoram, and pepper, beating until well blended. Add flour mixture a little at a time, mixing thoroughly after each addition.

Butter and flour two loaf pans. Spoon batter into pans, smooth tops, and bake 40 minutes or until a tester comes out clean. Cool 10 minutes and remove from pan.

MAKES 2 LOAVES.

SQUASH MUFFINS

Squash purée and chopped dates give these muffins a rich, sweet taste, great for breakfast. The purée should be relatively dry. If yours is more like applesauce, heat it gently in a wide saucepan or skillet until it begins to stick to the bottom. Stir frequently so that it doesn't scorch.

2 cups flour

2 teaspoons baking powder

1 teaspoon baking soda

1/2 teaspoon salt

1 teaspoon cinnamon

1/2 teaspoon ground ginger

2 eggs

1/2 cup yogurt

1/4 cup light oil

3/4 cup light brown sugar

1 cup fresh squash or pumpkin purée

1/2 cup coarsely chopped dates

Preheat oven to 450° F. Combine flour, baking powder, baking soda, salt, cinnamon, and ginger in a large bowl. Beat eggs and yogurt together in a separate bowl; beat in oil and brown sugar. Stir in squash or pumpkin purée and mix thoroughly. Add to dry ingredients and mix well. Stir in dates. Pour into well-greased muffin tins and bake 20 to 25 minutes.

MAKES 12 MUFFINS.

QUICK HERBED BISCUITS

When it comes to biscuits, I am very willing to sacrifice uniformity for speed. These little gems require no kneading or rolling and are none the worse for looking rough-cut. If you prefer rolled biscuits, decrease the milk to ¾ cup and proceed as usual.

1¼ cup all-purpose white flour

½ cup whole wheat flour

3 teaspoons baking powder

½ teaspoon salt

4 tablespoons butter or shortening, chilled

1 cup milk

¼ cup watercress leaves, chopped very fine

1 tablespoon chopped parsley

1 tablespoon chopped chives

Preheat oven to 450°F. Sift flours, baking powder, and salt into a bowl. Cut in butter or shortening until mixture resembles coarse cornmeal. Make a well in the center and pour in milk. Stir briefly, and then stir in watercress, parsley, and chives. Drop dough by spoonfuls onto a greased baking sheet. Bake 10 to 12 minutes or until lightly browned.

MAKES 18 SMALL BISCUITS.

MAPLE CARROT LOAF CAKE

This substantial cake has a firm texture and a warm maple taste. It travels well and makes a great treat for a skiing trip or sledding party.

¼ cup butter

2 cups grated carrot, lightly packed

1½ cups dry fine whole wheat bread crumbs

½ cup unsweetened shredded coconut

1 teaspoon cinnamon

½ teaspoon ground cloves

¼ teaspoon salt

1½ teaspoons vanilla

4 eggs, separated

⅓ cup maple syrup

1½ teaspoons vanilla

Preheat oven to 350°F. Melt butter in a medium skillet or saucepan. Add carrot and sauté until softened, about 5 minutes. Remove from heat. Combine bread crumbs, coconut, cinnamon, cloves, and salt in a mixing bowl. Stir in carrots. Beat maple syrup, egg yolks, and vanilla together and blend into carrot mixture.

Whip egg whites until stiff peaks form. Fold gently into carrot mixture and spread batter in a greased 5-by-9-inch loaf pan. Bake until a tester in the center comes out clean, about 35 to 40 minutes. Remove from pan and cool on rack.

MAKES ONE 5-BY-9-INCH LOAF.

CARROT DATE SQUARES

These are sensational. Make them in a smaller pan if you want a cakier texture.

6 tablespoons melted butter

1 cup flour

1 cup sugar

1/2 teaspoon baking soda

1/4 teaspoon salt

1 teaspoon ground cinnamon

1/4 teaspoon freshly grated nutmeg

1/4 teaspoon ground ginger

1 large egg, beaten

1/2 cup plain yogurt

1/2 teaspoon vanilla

1 cup shredded carrots

1/2 cup coarsely chopped dates

Heat oven to 375°F. Grease an 11-by-14-inch baking dish. In large mixing bowl, combine flour, sugar, baking soda, and salt. Add cinnamon, nutmeg, and ginger and blend thoroughly. Gradually stir in melted butter. Add egg, yogurt, and vanilla. Blend well.

Stir in carrots and dates and pour into prepared pan. Bake 25 to 30 minutes or until a tester comes out clean. Cool briefly on rack and serve warm or cool.

MAKES ONE LARGE PAN.

PUMPKIN COFFEE CAKE

Pumpkin pie filling goes on top of a layer of sweet batter, with streusel topping over all. This quick sweet is simple to make, but it does use lots of bowls.

2 cups flour

½ cup granulated sugar

1½ teaspoons baking powder

1 teaspoon salt, divided

6 tablespoons butter

3 eggs

⅓ cup milk

2¼ cups pumpkin purée

1 teaspoon cinnamon

½ teaspoon ground allspice

½ teaspoon ground ginger

½ cup plus 2 tablespoons light brown sugar, divided

½ teaspoon freshly grated nutmeg

Preheat oven to 350°F. Grease a 9-by-13-inch baking dish. Combine flour, white sugar, baking powder, and ½ teaspoon of the salt in a large bowl. Blend thoroughly. Cut in butter until mixture is crumbly. Take out half the mixture and put it in another bowl.

Beat 1 egg and milk in a separate bowl. Pour over one portion of the pastry mixture and toss with fork until moistened. Pat gently into baking dish and bake for 10 minutes. Remove from oven.

In yet another bowl, combine pumpkin purée, remaining 2 eggs, cinnamon, allspice, ginger, and remaining ½ teaspoon salt. Add ¼ cup of the brown sugar and blend well. Pour mixture over the cooked crust. Stir nutmeg and remaining brown sugar into reserved flour mixture and toss with fork. Sprinkle over filling. Bake for 30 to 40 minutes or until filling is set. Cool until filling is firm.

MAKES ONE
9-BY-13-INCH CAKE.

FRUIT PIZZA

You need a soft pear for this not-too-sweet pastry. Comices and Anjous are good choices. It can also be made with apples, and in the summertime with strawberries or apricots.

Dough

5 tablespoons milk

1 teaspoon yeast

2½ cups unbleached all-purpose flour

1 large egg

½ cup sugar

¼ cup softened butter

Scald milk and cool to tepid. Add yeast and set aside for 10 minutes. When yeast mixture is bubbling, combine with flour, egg, sugar, and butter. Turn onto a lightly floured board and knead about 5 minutes. Put dough in a large bowl, cover, and let rise in a warm, draft-free place until double, about 2 hours.

Filling

½ cup raisins

½ cup fresh orange juice, divided

4 tablespoons Cointreau or Grand Marnier, divided

3 ripe pears

⅓ cup pine nuts

Put raisins in small mixing bowl. Add 3 tablespoons of the orange juice and 1 tablespoon of the Cointreau or Grand Marnier and set aside. Peel and core pears and cut into wedges ¼ inch thick. Mix gently with remaining orange juice and liqueur and marinate for 1 hour.

Preheat oven to 375°F. Lightly butter an 8-by-12-inch baking dish. Punch dough down and shape into a ball. Roll it out on a lightly floured board until it is roughly the size of the baking dish. Place in dish and spread with your fingers to cover the entire bottom. Drain pears and distribute over dough, overlapping wedges attractively. Drain raisins and sprinkle, along with pine nuts, over the pears and between the rows. Bake 30 to 45 minutes, until crust is cooked and pears are golden brown. Serve at room temperature.

SERVES 8 TO 10.

CRANBERRY APPLE ROLL
RULET S KLYUKVOI

A nice addition to a holiday buffet, this Russian braided pastry combines a tart fruit filling with a rich crust. The pastry can also be used for piroshki.

Pastry

¾ cup butter, at room temperature

6 ounces cream cheese, at room temperature

1 egg yolk

1½ cups flour

¼ teaspoon salt

Cream butter and cream cheese together in a medium bowl. Beat in egg yolk. With your hands, work flour and salt into butter mixture to make a soft dough. Shape into a ball, wrap in waxed paper, and chill at least 30 minutes.

Filling

1 cup cranberries

½ cup sugar

2 tablespoons honey

1 tablespoon water

grated peel of 1 lemon

2 tablespoons flour

¼ teaspoon cinnamon

2 large tart apples, pared, cored, and chopped fine

1 egg yolk, beaten

Place cranberries, sugar, honey, water, lemon peel, flour, and cinnamon in a heavy saucepan. Bring to a boil and cook, stirring, about 10 minutes or until cranberries burst. Remove from heat and stir in apples.

Roll dough out and trim it to a 9-by-18-inch rectangle. Leaving a 3-inch strip down the center, cut strips about 1½ inches wide, radiating out from the center down both sides of the dough. A fluted pastry cutter makes a nice design. You should end up with a 3-inch-wide center strip and approximately 12 ribbons of dough on either side.

Spread filling along center strip. Then, alternating sides, fold in the strips at an angle, each one overlapping the next, so that the filling is completely covered. Transfer the roll to a greased baking sheet, using two spatulas. Brush with beaten egg yolk.

Bake approximately 1 hour at 375°F. Cover with foil toward the end so that it doesn't brown too much. Transfer the roll to a rack while still slightly warm. Serve at room temperature.

SERVES 8 TO 10.

NOCCIOLETTE

On my first trip to Italy, at age 7, I fell in love with hazelnut ice cream. Much later I learned to make these wonderful little cookies. They are more refined if you skin the nuts, but they are still great and a lot faster if you don't, provided the nuts are fresh; the skin gets bitter on nuts that have been around too long.

½ cup butter, at room temperature

⅔ cup powdered sugar, divided

1 cup flour

½ cup shelled hazelnuts, toasted, skinned (preferably), and coarsely ground

1½ tablespoons honey

Preheat oven to 350° F. Grease a baking sheet. Cream butter with ⅓ cup of the powdered sugar in large bowl until light and fluffy. Add flour, nuts, and honey and beat until smooth.

With lightly floured hands, form dough into ½-inch balls and space them 1 inch apart on baking sheet. Bake until firm, about 15 to 20 minutes. Transfer to rack until cool enough to handle and then roll in the remaining powdered sugar. Store in an airtight container.

MAKES 2½ DOZEN.

CARROT TORTE

Italians make this flourless cake with almonds. I like it with hazelnuts. The finer you grate the carrots, the more delicate the result will be. The carrots for this recipe can be ugly, but they must be sweet; don't use corky old ones.

3 cups grated carrots

9 tablespoons sugar

4 eggs, separated

2 cups lightly roasted hazelnuts or almonds, ground

¼ teaspoon allspice

2 teaspoons Marsala (optional)

whipped cream (optional)

Preheat oven to 275°F. Combine sugar and egg yolks and beat until thickened. Stir in carrots, hazelnuts or almonds, allspice, and Marsala (if used).

Beat egg whites until stiff and fold gently into carrot-nut mixture. Pour gently into a buttered 9-inch pie pan, smooth top, and bake for 1 hour. Serve lukewarm, possibly with Marsala-flavored whipped cream.

SERVES 6.

DRIED FRUIT TART WITH PINE NUTS

The concentrated flavors give this Provençal dessert a real impact. Just a delicious sliver is enough. The sweetness of the dried fruit means you need no sugar beyond what's in the jam. This recipe is from Mediterranean Harvest. I like to leave the apricots whole, for looks.

Pastry

2½ cups unbleached flour

¼ cup sugar

pinch of salt

6 tablespoons unsalted butter

2 large eggs, slightly beaten

1 tablespoon lemon juice

2 tablespoons water

Combine flour, sugar, and salt in a medium bowl. Add butter in small pieces and combine until mixture is crumbly. Add eggs, lemon juice, and water and mix together. The butter will still be a bit lumpy. Turn dough onto a lightly floured surface and knead lightly, just until butter is incorporated into flour. Roll dough into a ball, wrap with waxed paper, and chill at least 1 hour.

Filling

15 large prunes

25 dried apricots

3 tablespoons butter

grated rind of 1 lemon

5 tablespoons apricot jam

1¼ cups pine nuts

1 egg yolk, beaten

1 tablespoon water

Soak prunes and apricots for at least 6 hours in water to cover. Drain and squeeze out excess water. Pit prunes, chop fine, and combine with whole apricots. Blend butter with lemon rind and set aside.

Preheat oven to 350°F and butter a 10-inch pie pan. Reserve a small piece of dough (about ⅕ of the total) and roll out the rest about ⅛ inch thick. Line bottom and sides of pan with dough, allowing extra to drape over the sides. Pierce dough several times with a fork. Spread jam evenly over the surface. (If jam is very thick, dilute with a tablespoon of water.) Distribute chopped fruit over jam, dot with butter and lemon rind, and sprinkle pine nuts over the top. Roll out remaining dough, cut into ½-inch-wide strips, and make a lattice crust.

Combine egg yolk and water and brush mixture over top of dough. Bake until crust is golden and pine nuts are brown, about 40 minutes. Serve at room temperature.

SERVES 6 TO 8.

APPLE APPLESAUCE PIE

One day I set out to make Mrs. Anderson's Sour Cream Apple Pie (the recipe is in Lila Gault's Northwest Cookbook *and it's great) and found I didn't have any sour cream. The following improvisation is a bit easier on the arteries, and it got raves. I hate making pie crust so I use a pat-in-the-pan kuchen pastry whenever possible.*

Pastry

1³/₄ cups unbleached flour

¹/₄ teaspoon baking powder

1 tablespoon sugar

¹/₃ cup butter or butter and margarine mixture

Sift flour, baking powder, and sugar into a bowl. Add shortening, cut into small pieces, and blend with a fork or your fingers until it resembles coarse cornmeal. Press mixture into a pie pan and bake 10 minutes at 400°F. Remove from oven and cool before filling.

Filling

2¹/₂ to 3 cups apples, peeled, cored, and thinly sliced

2 tablespoons flour

¹/₂ teaspoon salt

³/₄ cup sugar

¹/₂ cup unsweetened yogurt

¹/₂ cup applesauce

1 egg, lightly beaten

¹/₂ teaspoon vanilla

Preheat oven to 375°. Place apples in pie shell. Combine flour, salt, and sugar in a medium bowl. Add yogurt, applesauce, egg, and vanilla and mix well. Pour over apples and bake for about 30 minutes or until mixture has set.

SERVES 6.

HAZELNUT PIE

This is the Northwest's answer to pecan pie. The recipe is from Gerald and Natalie Holmquist, who have a small commercial hazelnut orchard in northwest Washington. I can hardly overemphasize how good it is.

2 eggs

½ cup sugar

pinch salt

¾ cup dark corn syrup

1 tablespoon melted butter

½ teaspoon vanilla

2 cups finely chopped roasted hazelnuts

pastry for single-crust 9-inch pie

Preheat oven to 325°F. Beat eggs in medium bowl. Add in order sugar, salt, corn syrup, melted butter, and vanilla. Mix until blended and then stir in hazelnuts. Pour into pie shell and bake 50 to 60 minutes.

MAKES ONE 9-INCH PIE.

PUMPKIN PIE

Any favorite pie recipe is fine for making pumpkin pie from scratch. The trick is to minimize the hassle of preparing the purée. A good-sized pumpkin will make several pies. I freeze the purée in pie-sized portions, making it—after the initial labor—as convenient as canned. These instructions also apply to squash pies. As specialty squashes proliferate, the possibilities for variations in pie flavor also expand. You could have a pie tasting with several different varieties. Pumpkin pie recipes also make perfectly good custards. Just heat the oven heat to 350°F and set the custard dish in a pan of hot water.

Preparing the purée

Cut pumpkin in half and scrape out seeds and strings. (I am usually too impatient to clean and toast the seeds for a snack, but my daughter likes that job.) Place the halves cut side down on a cookie sheet or in a roasting pan. Don't use a rimless baking sheet because the pumpkins will ooze as they cook. Bake at 325°F until pumpkin is squishy when poked. It should be really soft but not beginning to burn.

Remove from oven and let cool a bit. Pour off the collected pumpkin juice and save. Peel the pumpkin, or scoop out the insides with a spoon. Purée the flesh bit by bit in a blender, adding some of the juice whenever needed. Get the mixture really smooth. Measure out a pie's worth of purée and freeze or can the rest. Then you are ready to proceed with your favorite recipe, or with the following one.

OLGA HEMMESTAD'S PUMPKIN PIE

Years ago the Bellingham Farmers Market had a pumpkin pie contest. Mrs. Hemmestad, an energetic testimony to the excellence of her own cooking at age 90, won with this recipe. It is not highly spiced, which allows you to appreciate the subtleties of your homegrown squash.

1½ cups half-and-half

¼ teaspoon maple extract

¾ cup light brown sugar

½ teaspoon salt

½ teaspoon cinnamon

¼ teaspoon nutmeg

¼ teaspoon ginger

1½ cups pumpkin, cooked and puréed

3 whole eggs, beaten

pastry for single-crust 9-inch pie

Preheat oven to 400°F. Bring half-and-half to a boil, remove from heat, and add maple extract. Combine all other ingredients and add to the half-and-half. Mix well. Pour into pie shell and bake about 40 minutes.

SERVES 6.

PUMPKIN AND PRUNE PIE

Elizabeth David helped introduce English-speaking cooks to Continental cuisines, including recipes for that New World transplant, the pumpkin. You may not recognize your old Thanksgiving standby without its familiar spices. A sweet winter squash such as Delicata can be substituted for pumpkin, and it should be if your only pumpkin is a jack-o'-lantern giant. If I didn't grow my own pie pumpkins, I wouldn't bother with fresh pumpkin anyway; canned purée is just fine for pies and custards.

1 pound pumpkin, peeled and chopped into 1-inch sections, or 1½ cups puréed pumpkin

3 tablespoons butter

20 prunes, pitted and soaked until soft

1 cup half-and-half

4 tablespoons sugar

pastry for double-crust 9-inch pie

Preheat oven to 400°F. Melt butter in a medium skillet and cook pumpkin gently until it is reduced to a purée. Remove from heat, add prunes, half-and-half, and sugar and mix well.

Line pie dish with bottom crust, put in filling, and cover with top crust. Bake 10 minutes at 400°. Lower heat to 350° and bake another 30 minutes.

SERVES 6.

RUTABAGA PIE

This recipe is from Maine, home of the great-tasting Laurentian rutabaga. If I didn't know what I was eating, I would think it was a pumpkin pie with an extra pinch of cloves. It's really good, and rutabagas are certainly more convenient than fresh pumpkin for peeling and puréeing. If you grow your own rutabagas, harvest after a frost and your pie will be that much better.

2 medium rutabagas

1 cup light brown sugar

2 tablespoons maple syrup

2 eggs, lightly beaten

1¼ cups half-and-half

½ teaspoon ginger

1 teaspoon cinnamon

½ teaspoon nutmeg

½ teaspoon cloves

½ teaspoon salt

1 teaspoon vanilla

pastry for single-crust 9-inch pie

Preheat oven to 450°F. Peel rutabagas and cut into chunks. Cook in a minimum of gently boiling water until soft, 25 to 30 minutes. Drain. Purée rutabagas in a blender. You should have 1½ cups. Add all remaining ingredients and blend until smooth. Pour into pastry shell.

Bake 15 minutes at 450°, reduce heat to 350°, and bake another 40 minutes or until mixture is set.

SERVES 6.

SPINACH TART

I first tried this unusual combination many years ago at Seattle's Raison d'Etre coffeehouse. Its fresh taste makes a nice change from the winter round of pumpkin and apple pies. Spinach desserts reportedly date back to the time of the Renaissance, when French and English cooks began exploring the possibilities of the vegetable, newly arrived from Spain. A regional variation is sorrel pie, a specialty of the Blasket Islands off the coast of Ireland.

1 cup milk or half-and-half

2 eggs

⅓ cup sugar

2 cups cooked spinach, drained

grated rind of 1 small lemon

1 teaspoon vanilla

½ cup apricot jam

pastry for single-crust 9-inch pie, plus extra for lattice if desired

Preheat oven to 450°F. Blend milk or half-and-half, eggs, and sugar in top of a double boiler. Cook slowly, stirring constantly, until mixture thickens enough to coat the spoon. Chop spinach, press dry, and stir into custard with lemon rind and vanilla. Melt jam in a small saucepan over low heat.

Spoon half of spinach mixture into pie shell. Cover with ⅓ cup of the jam, then the rest of the spinach, and then the remainder of the jam. Add a lattice top crust if you wish.

Bake 20 minutes. Serve at room temperature.

SERVES 6.

CÔTE D'AZUR TART

◆ *If you like the Spinach Tart, you can move on to an even odder combination of Swiss chard, apples, raisins, and Parmesan cheese. This recipe is from* Mediterranean Harvest, *which is a wonderful resource for adventurous cooks.*

⅓ cup pine nuts, lightly toasted

1½ cups chopped chard

2 tablespoons currants or raisins, soaked in 3 tablespoons dark rum for 20 minutes

2 eggs, beaten

½ cup sugar

¼ cup grated Parmesan cheese

pinch of black pepper

3 cups peeled, cored, and sliced apples or firm pears

pastry for a double-crust 9-inch pie

Preheat oven to 375°F. Toast pine nuts lightly in an ungreased skillet over medium heat and set aside.

Bring 1 cup of water to a boil in a medium saucepan, add chard, and cook, covered, over medium heat for 10 minutes. Drain and squeeze out all excess water once chard is cool enough to handle. Combine all remaining ingredients except the apples in a large mixing bowl, then blend in the chard.

Smooth chard mixture evenly across bottom of pie shell and cover with apple slices. Roll out remaining dough and cover pie, pressing to join edges. Prick top crust to let steam escape. Bake for 50 minutes to 1 hour, until crust is browned and filling firm. Cover top crust with foil if it browns before filling is ready. Serve warm or at room temperature.

SERVES 6.

APPLE-ALMOND CRISP

This is a slightly fancier version of good old apple crisp. The more flavorful the apples, the better the result.

2½ pounds (about 6 medium) tart cooking apples

¾ cup plus 2 tablespoons sugar, divided

1 tablespoon fresh lemon juice

1 cup flour

¼ teaspoon ground cinnamon

⅔ cup chopped blanched almonds

1 teaspoon vanilla

½ cup butter, melted

whipped cream (optional)

Preheat oven to 400°F. Butter a 9-by-13-inch baking dish. Peel and core apples and slice lengthwise, 1 inch thick. Put sliced apples, lemon juice, and the 2 tablespoons sugar in a bowl and toss. Arrange apple slices in rows in baking dish, overlapping slightly.

Sift together flour, the remaining ¾ cup sugar, and cinnamon. Stir in almonds. Add vanilla to melted butter and drizzle over almond mixture, tossing with a fork until crumbly. Sprinkle mixture over apples.

Bake until apples are tender and topping is browned, about half an hour. The apples should not turn to mush. Serve warm, with whipped cream on the side if you like.

SERVES 8.

APPLE PASTILA

◈ *This 19th-century Russian confection smells heavenly while it is cooking. The meringues will be alarmingly chewy when they come out of the oven but will turn crisp and light as they dry.*

3 large, tart apples

1 teaspoon fresh lemon juice

1 cup sugar

¼ teaspoon almond extract

¼ teaspoon cinnamon

2 egg whites

flour

Peel, halve, and core apples, and steam over boiling water until tender. Purée apples and pour into a large bowl. Stir in lemon juice, sugar, almond extract, and cinnamon.

Beat egg whites until stiff but not dry. Stir into apple mixture. Beat at high speed for at least 5 minutes, or for 10 to 15 minutes by hand. Preheat oven to 150° F. Spread a sheet of aluminum foil on a baking sheet. Grease lightly and dust with flour. Drop the apple foam by tablespoonfuls onto the foil.

Bake about 6 hours, until confections are dry to the touch. Transfer to a wire rack to cool. Keep in a tightly closed container until just before serving.

MAKES ABOUT 5 DOZEN.

CARROT HALVAH

Indian cooking includes an array of milk-based sweets, many of them the province of professional candy cooks. However, this simple version is generally made at home. It is much moister than the ground-sesame halvah sold in this country, and it does not keep as long. (The latter has not been a problem at our house.) Whole cardamom and unsalted butter do make a difference in this recipe.

3 cups milk

½ cup brown sugar (the unrefined brown sugar now sold in some supermarkets is the closest to Indian sugar)

2 cups coarsely grated carrots (3 or 4 medium)

10 pods cardamom (about ½ teaspoon ground)

½ cup unsalted butter or ghee (page 218)

½ cup almonds, chopped

½ cup raisins

¼ teaspoon mace

2 tablespoons honey

Bring milk to a boil in a heavy saucepan. Add brown sugar and carrots. Return to boil, reduce to just below the boiling point, and cook, uncovered, for 45 minutes, stirring often to keep carrots from sticking. The liquid should reduce by at least half and the mixture should be quite thick.

Take cardamom seeds from their pods and crush them with a rolling pin or a mortar and pestle. Melt butter in a large frying pan and sauté almonds and raisins for 2 minutes. Add cardamom and mace to frying pan and stir well. Stir in honey and cook another minute. Pour in milk and carrot mixture and bring to a boil. Cook, stirring constantly, until halvah begins to stiffen and pull away from the sides of the pan.

Remove from heat, spoon into a shallow, flat dish, and smooth top. Let cool before serving. Refrigerate for an hour if you want to cut the halvah into the traditional diamond shapes.

SERVES 8.

PEARS IN SYRUP

There are lots of good recipes for poached pears. This is one of the oldest, tracing its lineage to a medieval dish that used vinegar rather than wine. It's a good use for Seckel pears, an heirloom variety that shows up in many old orchards and sometimes in stores. Seckels are small and brownish green, with long necks. The ones in my pasture are ready in October and keep about a month. They taste quite a lot like those pricey round Asian pears, being hard and not particularly sweet. I don't care for them fresh, but they are great for cooking.

6 Seckel or Bosc pears

⅔ cup sugar

up to 1 bottle of dry red wine

1-by-3-inch section orange rind

1 stick cinnamon

6 whole cloves

three ¼-inch slices fresh ginger

4 threads saffron (optional)

whipped cream or custard sauce

Peel pears, leaving stems on. Stand them upright in a deep, narrow earthenware or enamel casserole with cover. Add sugar and enough wine to cover halfway. Tie orange rind, cinnamon, cloves, ginger, and saffron (if used) in cheesecloth and add to casserole. Add enough water to cover pears.

Cover casserole and bake at 250°F for 5 to 7 hours, basting pears occasionally as liquid cooks down. Bake until liquid is a rich syrup and pears are completely tender but not falling apart. Cool in syrup. Remove spice bag and serve pears with whipped cream or custard sauce.

SERVES 6.

CARROT-PARSNIP CUSTARD

You could make this with 3 cups of carrots and no parsnips, but the combination gives a nice blend in both flavor and color. After years of frustration trying to get a custard dish into a pan of boiling water without burning myself or splashing my creation, I found the answer. Place the custard dish in a deep empty pan—I use a soup kettle—and then stick a funnel between dish and kettle and pour the boiling water through it. Maybe you already knew that.

4 tablespoons butter

2 cups finely grated carrots

1 cup finely grated parsnips

¼ cup flour

1 teaspoon salt

½ teaspoon ground ginger

3 eggs, lightly beaten

⅓ cup maple syrup

1½ cups half-and-half

Preheat oven to 325°F. Melt butter in a large saucepan, add carrots and parsnips, and sauté gently for about 5 minutes, until vegetables begin to soften. Remove from heat. Combine flour, salt, and ginger and stir mixture into vegetables. Add eggs, maple syrup, and half-and-half and stir well.

Pour into buttered custard dish and set in pan of boiling water. Water should always be about 1 inch up on sides of dish. Add more boiling water while baking, if necessary. Bake until knife inserted in center comes out clean, about 1½ to 2 hours.

SERVES 6.

CRANBERRY MACAROON CREAM

Tart cranberries and rich macaroons are a surprising combination. I make this in November with the last mint of the season. Cranberries are easier to chop when they are partly frozen.

1 cup whipping cream

½ cup sugar

6 ounces cranberries (half a package)

4 teaspoons chopped fresh mint leaves

1½ cups crumbled coconut macaroons

Whip cream until stiff, adding sugar gradually. Chop cranberries by hand or in blender. Stir cranberries and mint leaves into whipped cream. Add macaroons, stir carefully, and chill at least an hour.

SERVES 4.

QUINCE SORBET

Robin Saunders, co-owner of Le Gourmand in Seattle, provided the recipe for this tangy golden sorbet.

1 cup water

2 cups sugar

2 large (apple-sized) quinces

half an egg white, lightly beaten

Boil water and sugar to make a thin syrup. Remove from heat and let cool. Peel and seed quinces, slice, and place in saucepan with just enough water to keep from burning. Cook, covered, until soft. Remove from heat and purée. You should have 1½ cups. Cool, and then add ⅔ cup of the syrup and the egg white. Process in an ice cream maker.

MAKES 1 PINT.

ROSE PEAR GRANITA

No special equipment is required for this simple ice from Le Gourmand. The rose hips give the crystals a bit of tartness and a gorgeous red-gold tint. This makes a good digestive as well as a deceptively simple dessert.

1 quart pear juice

½ cup rose hips, cut in half and seeded

Pour juice into a saucepan, add rose hips, and simmer, covered, until liquid is reduced by half. Put through a food mill and pour into a shallow pan. Freeze. Stir when mixture starts to get slushy and return to freezer until time to serve.

MAKES 1 PINT.

HAZELNUT ROCA

The year I made this with nuts from our own trees and butter from our own cow, I felt I had reached the pinnacle of country living. Now I'm back to storebought ingredients, but this candy is still a favorite addition to the Christmas cookie plate.

½ pound unsalted butter

½ cup chopped hazelnuts

½ cup ground hazelnuts

1 cup sugar

one 6-ounce package semisweet chocolate chips

Melt butter over high heat in a cast-iron skillet or other heavy, shallow pan. Add sugar, bit by bit, as butter is melting. Stir constantly but gently. When sugar starts to change color, add chopped hazelnuts. Stir and test for hard crack stage in cold water. Pour into a shallow pan and cool. (Any "runoff" of melted butter from the cooling candy can be poured off and saved to use in other baking. It has a wonderful flavor.) Score the candy lightly before it's fully cool so it will be easier to break into tidy pieces.

Melt chocolate chips in a double boiler over simmering water. Stir in ground hazelnuts and spread chocolate mixture over the cooled candy. When cold, break into pieces.

MAKES 30 1-BY-2-INCH CANDIES.

MENUS

MENUS

Root vegetable and leek soup with Gouda cheese
Escarole and cabbage salad
Rye bread
Beer, cider

Tempura with dipping sauce
rice
Shikumchee
Kimpira gobo
Sake, beer, Japanese tea

Mushroom soup
Endive and watercress salad
Celeriac and cheese purée
Bread
Apple-almond crisp
Beaujolais

Baked fish and chicory
Risotto with chestnuts
Mixed green salad
Carrot torte
Soave

Broccoli dal curry
Indian spinach with potatoes
Carrot curry
Basmati rice
Radish raita
Chapati or pita bread
Carrot halvah
Tea, beer

Roast chicken with Baked parsnips
Brussels sprout salad
Steamed carrots
Herb biscuits
Cranberry macaroon cream

Corn salad and arugula with beets
Grilled fish with mint chutney
Georgian-style cauliflower
Bulgur
Hazelnut pie

Jerusalem artichoke soup Provençale
Rice
Swiss chard and olives
Fruit pizza

Ethiopian collards and cottage cheese
Pumpkin-cheese pancakes
Antibes coleslaw
Beer, fruit juice, tea

Antipasto of carrots, small leeks, broccoli,
and turnips, or mixed green salad
Whole wheat pasta with onion sauce
Beef with cardoons and mushrooms
Bread
Valpolicella

OUTDOOR EATING

Italian spinach and rice pie
Maple carrot loaf cake or Nocciolette
Local apples and Comice pears
Cheese

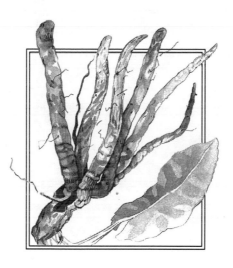

INDOOR GARDENING

INDOOR GROWING

If you live in a moderate climate and have a garden, you can grow the vegetables presented in this book. Only a truly obsessive person would attempt to grow them all in any one year, but you can have a variety of produce year-round. I highly recommend *Winter Gardening in the Maritime Northwest* (Sasquatch Books, 1989), by Binda Colebrook, for all aspiring winter gardeners. If you are a dedicated gardener but your winter weather is severe, *Intensive Gardening Round the Year* by P. Doscher, T. Fisher, and K. Kolb (Stephen Greene Press, 1983) is a good resource for working with cold frames, greenhouses, and heat-conserving devices.

It also is possible to grow winter produce indoors. Because your space will be limited, you will want to concentrate on hard-to-find vegetables and ones for which freshness is most crucial. This brief guide will concentrate on the low-tech end of the indoor spectrum, without special lights, heat cables, or other aids. Growing under artificial light is a big subject, and I don't know much about it. Check the titles in References at the end of this section for guidance, or head down to your local halide light shop for a chat. They'll be glad to see a licit customer.

The single biggest problem in indoor growing, especially in winter, is light, although humidity and temperature also can cause problems. I wish I had a dollar (or a sunny day) for every time I've read instructions to place my pots where they will get several hours of daily sunshine. I would have to move my windowsills to another state. Pacific Northwest gardeners are already used to having crops take much longer to mature than most seed catalogs claim. Copywriters' hyperbole is responsible for part of this discrepancy, but cloudy maritime summers are a big factor. Most seed companies test their products in sunnier climes. This problem is accentuated indoors in winter, and harvest times must be pushed back accordingly even for shade-tolerant plants such as lettuce.

Indoor humidity also is likely to be lower than many plants like, and sharp changes in temperature can be stressful, especially for seedlings. The combination of warm, dry daytime air and low light levels can push a young plant into trying to grow too fast for the photosynthetic energy available to it. The result is a spindly, pale specimen that tastes better to pests than it does to you. But like a lot of houseplants, vegetables do need to grow to be of any use.

Getting started

All these obstacles place a premium on details. You can grow vegetables on your windowsill, but you need to pay close attention to fertility, hygiene, and selection. In general, your best bets are leaf crops. Roots and flowers take more of the plant's energy to produce.

Since you will be growing outside the standard commercial season, your sources for started plants may be limited. If you do find seedlings for sale, or if a gardening friend will provide starts, take them. You'll be over the first big hurdle. Otherwise, use extra care in germinating seeds indoors. Individual pots and shallow trays of soil are vulnerable. They get waterlogged quickly and they dry out quickly—and either extreme can be fatal quickly. I hate to think how many seedlings I've lost to damping-off disease, probably the biggest scourge of the indoor seed starter. Damping-off is a waterborne mold (genus *Pythium*) that thrives in wet soil, especially when low light levels make seedlings less vigorous. The new little stem gets thin just above the soil line and the baby plant falls over.

There is no cure for damping-off, so you must concentrate on prevention. Use new or well-cleaned pots and sterile starting medium. Make sure soil is well drained and keep it moist, not soaking wet. If light is marginal, even a reading light or desk lamp will help to supplement what comes through the window. If plants start toppling despite all your care, discard the whole potful. It isn't worth spreading the mold just to save a few marginal specimens.

Soil

Although you will probably want to start your produce in a sterile potting medium, it will need first-rate soil to grow to harvest size. Indoor potting soils will be fine for most leaf crops, but you will need to provide extra phosphorus if you are growing carrots, beets, or other root crops. Bone meal, which I don't use outdoors because it costs too much, may be the best choice to supplement small amounts of indoor soil. Rock phosphate is cheaper and more pleasant to work with, but it releases slowly and you probably don't want 40 pounds of it in your condo closet. Other nitrogen-rich fertilizers I use outside, like manure tea and fish emulsions, are too smelly, and many handy tablet fertilizers for houseplants are too harsh. They act so fast that the plant may suffer leaf burn and other signs of excess. If you want a tablet fertilizer, try a slow-release product such as Sunrise Plant Food Tablets.

Containers

Most of the plants suitable for indoor growing do not have deep root systems and can be grown in relatively shallow containers. You don't need giant tubs, and in fact you can grow a surprising number of vegetables in 8-inch pots. If you use clay pots, you must be extra careful not to let the soil dry out; if you use plastic pots, you must watch out for overwatering. Clay is certainly more aesthetically pleasing, but plastic is easier to clean. The more surface area you have in relation to soil, the less forgiving your plants will be about watering lapses. That means that large containers are easier to deal with than small ones. Grouping a number of plants together also will help combat the low humidity that can desiccate tender new leaves.

Pests

Many bugs thrive indoors, where their normal predators can't find them. The ones that have given me the most trouble are aphids and red spider mites. Once again, hygiene helps. If they show up anyway, they can be sprayed off with a good jet of water, and even more effectively with a mixture of water and Safer's insecticidal soap, which is economical and safe. You can get Safer's, either in bulk or in a mister, at most garden stores or by mail order through seed catalogs. I don't recommend any stronger insecticides indoors. Harmful chemical levels can be reached very quickly in a well-insulated house.

What to grow

The list that follows is by no means inclusive. It features plants that you can reasonably expect to grow without a lot of equipment and that will yield results worth the effort.

Arugula

Arugula is a good indoor choice because freshness is crucial and only a few leaves are needed to brighten a salad. You can combine it in a pot with corn salad or grow it on its own. Temperatures above 70°F will result in a flavor that's too hot to handle. Arugula is very resistant to disease and can be grown under crowded conditions. Don't let the soil dry out.

Carrots

Among the few root crops worth trying indoors, really fresh carrots are wonderfully sweet. The best varieties don't store well and are seldom seen in stores. If you have a lot of light, you can treat yourself to the finest. Look for small, Nantes-type varieties or the ball-shaped Parmex (Johnny's Selected Seeds), whose roots are only two or three inches long. Carrots like being rather crowded, and you can grow small ones 1½ inches apart in an 8-inch pot. The seed takes a long time to germinate and is discouraged by crusty soil. A very light covering of sifted compost or sand is easy to keep moist but not soggy. Once up, carrots like rich, moist soil and relatively cool temperatures. A plus for indoor growers is that you won't have to worry about the rustfly maggot, a nasty pest that ruins a lot of winter carrots.

Corn salad

Corn salad can stand warmth as well as cold, so it can handle a variety of household conditions. It's an attractive little plant that could be seeded around the base of an indoor tree or other large specimen, as long as light reaches the pot and not just the leaves of the larger plant. Sow heavily and be patient. Germination takes time. You can eat the thinnings of the youngest plants, and the rest will grow larger to fill in the gaps.

Winter cress

Winter cress (not to be confused with watercress) needs temperatures below 70°F for best flavor; like a lot of peppery-tasting plants, it gets too hot in the heat. It is easy and quick to grow, producing edible leaves in a week to 10 days. If you have one of those hollow pottery animals sold for sprouting chia seeds, you can grow cress on it. Otherwise, a shallow tray, even an ice-cube tray, will give maximum production for a minimum of dirt. Don't combine it with other plants, because the constant harvesting will disturb its neighbors.

Escarole and chicory

These grow more slowly than lettuce, but the good news is that indoor plants will likely be less bitter than those grown outside. Start them in mid- to late summer, so they can get in some growth before the sun dims, and allow an 8-inch pot or equivalent for each mature plant.

Lettuce

You can always buy lettuce, but seed catalogs have an intoxicating array of specialty varieties that are worth trying indoors if you are serious about your salads. Some are so beautiful they rival standard foliage ornamentals. Lettuces grow relatively well, though slowly, in low light, but they are fussy about temperature and moisture. Too much warmth without enough light and they will get pale and spindly. Too moist and they acquire a variety of soilborne rots; too dry and they don't taste good. Try a buttercrunch or Bibb variety. Many lettuce types need light to germinate. You may need to keep them under a table lamp or other light source until they come up. Although summer lettuces are often grown close together in order to shade the soil, winter crops need a bit more room. Grow them one plant per 6-inch pot or equivalent, and fertilize often with a good source of nitrogen.

Asian greens

Any of the quick-growing mustards are worth a try inside. They are tolerant of low light, as long as they get enough water and not too much heat. Harvest can begin almost as soon as leaves appear. Many of the plants themselves are lovely, with frilly leaves that deserve a closer look. They can be grown three or four to a 6-inch pot.

Radishes

One good thing about an indoor radish is freedom from its two most devastating pests—slugs and rootfly maggots. Radishes grow fast and are happiest with cool temperatures and moist soil. They make a good project for kids, offering quick gratification and bright colors. "Easter egg" packages, sold by several seed companies, will give you a mixture of red, pink, white, and purple roots. Cool temperatures, preferably not above 60°F, are important for germination.

Watercress

Watercress takes some effort, but it's worth it if you are an enthusiast, because storebought quality is so variable and it keeps so poorly. Since watercress grows naturally in and near streams, the gardener's task is to provide constant moisture without stagnant water. Try sprouting seeds on damp paper and then moving them to sandy soil in a moss-lined pot. The sand helps with drainage, while the moss conserves moisture. Watercress doesn't like direct sun, so choose your window accordingly. Clip leaves and stems off the growing plants.

Sprouts

I confine my sprout-making to a few batches of alfalfa sprouts each winter, but that just scratches the surface of the fresh food you can produce with a minimum of labor and equipment. Soaking and rinsing requirements are different for the different beans and grains in the sprouters' cupboard, and I won't go into them here. See References for information.

Herbs

Herbs can tolerate the low humidity of most houses better than most vegetables can. Light levels are likely to be a bigger problem because a lot of our culinary herbs originate in sunny climes. A number of garden books advocate harsh treatment for herbs, on the theory that slower growth and poor soil concentrate their flavor. This could be a boon for the indoor grower, but I can't verify it. I have excellent soil, and my herbs taste fine to me. Within the limits of your household climate, the herbs to try indoors are the ones that are hard to find in stores or marginal in the winter garden. It's heartbreaking to lose a rosemary plant to a vicious storm when you could have been admiring it on the kitchen window.

Chervil

Chervil looks like very finely cut parsley and is in fact closely related. I have a lot of trouble growing it outdoors, and I think I'll try inside next, where I can keep a closer eye on it. It needs moisture (in both soil and air), good soil and drainage, and room to get about a foot tall. It doesn't require a lot of sun, and new seedlings in a bright window will need to be shaded.

Chives

Lots of people bring their chives in for the winter. It's gratifying to have a snip right there handy for your scrambled eggs or baked potatoes. Chives need a dormant period before being forced back into growth. Give them a month outdoors in cold weather or stick them in the refrigerator. Keep the soil well fertilized to give the plant energy to replace clipped leaves.

Rosemary

When I went to college in California, I lived in a house with a big rosemary shrub each side of the doorway. Here in Washington, I keep my well-loved plant in a pot so I can bring it in during fierce weather. Although it prefers lots of light, it tolerates my dim winter rooms.

Thyme

Thyme needs more indoor light than I've got. Otherwise I definitely would bring it in, because mine freezes out two winters out of three. Thyme needs an 8-inch pot, frequent fertilizing, and light soil. It likes humidity, but prefers soil a bit on the dry side. English and French thyme are the most versatile in the kitchen, but lemon thyme is still my favorite.

References

Rodale's Encyclopedia of Indoor Gardening
Anne Halpin, ed.
Emmaus, Penn.: Rodale Press, 1980

A very comprehensive book, with natural gardening orientation. The last thing you want added to the overused air of your home in winter, especially the kitchen, is a bunch of agricultural pesticides. My only complaint with Rodale's big books is that they sometimes seem overoptimistic.

The Contained Garden
Kenneth A. Beckett, David Carr, David Stevens
New York: Penguin Books, 1982

A beautiful paperback that makes you want to put all your plants in pots. It does not specifically address indoor growing but has extensive, specific information on containers, soil mixtures, and disease control for vegetables as well as ornamentals. This is the book I'll use if I ever switch to patio gardening.

The New Seed Starter's Handbook
Nancy Bubel
Emmaus, Penn.: Rodale Press, 1988

Covers all aspects of growing seedlings, with an organic gardener's orientation.

Raising Transplants at Home
Steve Solomon
Lorane, Ore.: Territorial Seed Company

Territorial founder and garden fanatic Steve Solomon addresses the problems of low light and germination temperatures that complicate indoor winter gardening.

SOURCES

The recipes in *Winter Harvest* come from a variety of cuisines. The following books are among my favorites for year-round cooking.

Africa News Cookbook: African Cooking for Western Kitchens
Africa News Service Inc., Tami Hultman, ed.
New York: Penguin Books, 1986

Good food and a fascinating book about some of the world's least-known cuisines.

Elizabeth David Classics
Elizabeth David
New York: Alfred A. Knopf Inc., 1980

A one-volume compilation of three groundbreaking books—*Mediterranean Food*, *French Country Cooking*, and *Summer Cooking*. These recipes, like purely literary classics, can be read as a statement of philosophy as much as for specific instruction. David scorns detailed directions and American measurements, often calling for a dessert-spoon of this and a gill of that. This can be frustrating, and you may want to hunt down more specific adaptations of some of her recipes. Still, nowhere else will you find so many classic country meals, and no one has matched the clarity, color, and passion that David brought to bear on the bleak landscape of postwar British cooking.

Fresh from France: Vegetable Creations
Faye Levy
New York: E. P. Dutton Inc., 1987

Classic French vegetable cookery, with lots of butter and cream but without a lot of fuss. These recipes are unintimidating, and all are designed to celebrate, not disguise, the vegetables they feature.

Indian Cooking
Khalid Aziz
New York: Perigee Books, 1983

Includes meat and seafood as well as vegetarian dishes. The recipes are clear and easy to follow, although you will have to allow for the British use of measurement by weight rather than volume. The food is delicious.

INDEX

A

I

Indian spinach with potatoes, 124
    to accompany, 172
Indoor growing, 257–262
    containers, 258–259
    damping-off disease, 258
    fertilizers, 258
    germinating seeds, 258
    herbs, 261–262
    humidity, 257
    light, 257
    pests, 259
    soil, 258
    temperature, 257
    vegetables, 259–261
Innisfree (restaurant), 69, 110
Innisfree Jerusalem artichoke soup, 69
Intensive Gardening Round the Year, 257
Inulin, 36, 48
Italian carrot marinade, 92
Italian greens and rice soup, 66
Italian sausage with fennel, carrot, and
    cabbage, 135
Italian spinach and rice pie, 131

J

James, Myrtle, 74
Jerusalem artichokes:
    about, 36
    as celeriac substitute, 63
    as parsnip substitute, 76, 197
    baked, with mushrooms, 119
    for dieting and diabetes, 36
    illus., 35
    in Brussels sprout salad, 88
    in cold weather, 12
    in sour cream, 187
    in stuffed savoy, 126
    in Sunday brunch frittata, 123
    in Turkish cauliflower and lentil stew, 109

    in winter-run soup, 80
    Innisfree, soup, 69
    pickled, 220
    Rutachoke salad, 101
    soup Provençale, 70
    with rice, 188
Johnny's Selected Seeds, 39, 259, 267
Johnson, Samuel, 40

K

Kale:
    about, 10, 36, 38
    as cardoon substitute, 169
    bacon, and potatoes, 133
    in brose, 71
    in caldo verde, 72
    in cold weather, 12
    in Southern mixed greens, 185
    in stampot, 200
    manicotti, 110
    Romeo Conca's pork chops and, 134
    sprouts, 189
Kemnitzer, John, 149
Kim chee:
    about and recipe, 167
    as sauerkraut substitute, 59
Kimpira gobo, 183
Kitchen equipment, 12
Koftesi, 201
Kohlrabi:
    about, 38
    as Brussels sprouts substitute, 164
    as celeriac substitute, 177
    as turnip substitute, 104
    baked, and fennel, 189
    illus., 37
    in bagna cauda, 156
    in kim chee, 167
    in soy sauce vegetables, 187
    salad, 95
Korean spinach and garlic, *see* Shikumchee
Kuchen pastry, 235

L

M

S

greens, 52
greens, as turnip substitute, 212
greens, in hortopita, 186
Hungarian, *see* Kohlrabi
in garbure, 61
in maple mustard sauce, 212
in soy sauce vegetables, 187
salad, 104
sauté of broccoli and, 163
with anchovies, 212
Tyfon, 40

V

Vegetables for tempura, 152
Vegetarian Epicure, The, 121, 266
Vichyssoise, 73
Vietnamese beef with leeks, 145
Vinaigrette dressing, on green salads, 97

W

Watercress:
   as sorrel substitute, 68
   endive and, salad, 94
   growing indoors, 261

in fennel and apple salad, 95
in quick herbed biscuits, 226
in salat, 101
in Thai beef and radish salad, 103
in Tibetan salad, 96
potato, purée, 198
raita, 100
Wilted greens salad, 98
Winter cress, 260
*Winter Gardening in the Maritime
   Northwest,* 9, 257
Winter-run soup, 80

XYZ

Yams:
   about, 10, 50–51
Yarrow Bay Grill, 149
Yogurt:
   broccoli, soup, 60
   in raitas, 100
   in Tibetan salad, 96
Zeytinyagli yer elmasiyra, 188
Zimino, 148
Zimmerman, Ron, 78
Zucchini, 10, 50

ABOUT THE AUTHOR

©Mary Randlett

Lane Morgan is a writer, teacher, editor, and avid gardener. She is the author of *Greetings from Washington* and *Seattle: A Pictorial History*. She is co-author, with her husband, Bruce Brown, of *The Miracle Planet*, the companion guide to the PBS series of the same name.

Lane lives with her family in Washington state near the Canadian border. She has been winter gardening on her small farm for many years, where she grows much of the produce mentioned in the *Winter Harvest Cookbook*.

DID YOU ENJOY THIS BOOK?

Sasquatch Books publishes cookbooks and travel guides related to the Pacific Northwest. Our books are available at bookstores and other retail outlets throughout the region. Here is a selection of current titles:

NORTHWEST BEST PLACES
Restaurants, Lodgings, and Touring in Oregon, Washington, and British Columbia
Edited by David Brewster and Stephanie Irving $15.95

SEATTLE BEST PLACES
A Discriminating Guide to Seattle's Restaurants, Lodgings, Shopping, Nightlife, Arts, Sights, Outings, and Annual Events
Edited by David Brewster and Kathryn Robinson $10.95

PORTLAND BEST PLACES
A Discriminating Guide to Portland's Restaurants, Lodgings, Shopping, Nightlife, Arts, Sights, Outings, and Annual Events
Edited by Stephanie Irving $10.95

BREAKFAST IN BED
The Best B&B Recipes from Northern California to British Columbia
by Carol Frieberg $14.95

Cooking with EIGHT ITEMS OR LESS
Great-Tasting Recipes for the Express Lane Gourmet
by Ann Lovejoy $11.95

To receive a Sasquatch Books catalog, or to inquire about ordering our books by phone or mail, please contact us at the address below.

SASQUATCH BOOKS   1931 Second Avenue, Seattle, WA 98101   (206) 441-5555